OPENING CREDITS

CW00434275

Contributors this issue: James Aaron, Simon J. Ballard, Rachel Bellwoar, Michael Campochiaro, Sebastian Corbascio, Dawn Dabell, Martin Dallard, David Flack, Shawn Gordon, John Harrison, Bryan C. Kuriawa, James Lecky, Ernie Magnotta, Peter Sawford, Joe Secrett, Ian Talbot Taylor, Dr Andrew C. Webber. Caricature artwork by Aaron Stielstra.

All articles, photographs and specially produced artwork remain copyright their respective author/photographer/artist. Opinions expressed herein are those of the individual.

Design and Layout: Dawn Dabell
Copy Editor: Jonathon Dabell

Most images in this magazine come from the private collection of Dawn and Jonathon Dabell, or the writer of the corresponding article. Those which do not are made available in an effort to advance understanding of cultural issues pertaining to academic research. We believe this constitutes 'fair use' of any such copyrighted material as provided for in Section 107 of the US Copyright Law. In accordance with Title U.S.C Section 107, this magazine is sold to those who have expressed a prior interest in receiving the included information for research, academic and educational purposes.

Printed globally by Amazon KDP

A Word from the Editing Room

Greetings!

Welcome to Issue 4 of 'Cinema of the '80s'. We're delighted to be back with more features and articles about the decade's films and film stars.

We must begin by welcoming two newcomers to our writing team. First, Ernie Magnotta who takes a look at the comedy classic *Caddyshack* (1980). Second, Shawn Gordon who provides a substantial analysis of the career of Charles Bronson during the period when he worked extensively for Menahem Golan and Yoram Globus at Cannon. Two fabulous and interesting articles, we hope you 'll agree.

There's plenty more to get your teeth into too, including pieces about *To Live and Die in L.A.* (1985), *Knightriders* (1981), *Runaway Train* (1985), *Heartbreak Ridge* (1986), *Greystoke: The Legend of Tarzan, Lord of the Apes* (1984) and much more.

It seems hard to believe that some of the films covered within our pages are already forty years old. Time and tide wait for no man, indeed! There will be readers who recall seeing these movies for the first time in movie theatres or on home video like it was yesterday. Sometimes, revisiting films several times over the years enables us to spot new details, to appreciate little quirks of acting or moments of dialogue or touches of camerawork that we may have failed to take in our first viewing. Time can make our love for a certain movie grow or wane. It's always fascinating to reflect the way something that once seemed brilliant may fall from grace, while something that once seemed terrible may prove far better than anyone at the time realised.

That's enough pre-ambling for now. Thanks again for supporting the mag. Enjoy Issue 4, and we hope to see you again when Issue 5 comes around.

Dawn and Jonathon Dabell

Remembering Treat Williams (1951 - 2023)

On June 12th, 2023, Treat Williams was killed in a motorcycle accident in Vermont. He was 71.

Williams came to distinction in the late '70s, featuring prominently in Steven Spielberg's *1941* (1979) and playing the lead role in Milos Forman's *Hair* (1979). He seemed to have superstardom at his fingertips and made a strong start to the '80s, further consolidating that promise, working with directing titans like Sidney Lumet and Sergio Leone. While he perhaps did not fulfil his star potential, he was nevertheless a major player of the era. He remained active until his death, enjoying recurring roles in hit TV shows like *Chesapeake Shores* and *Blue Bloods* as well as numerous film roles

His '80s films were:
The Empire Strikes Back (1980) (uncredited)
Why Would I Lie? (1980)
Prince of the City (1981)
The Pursuit of D.B. Cooper (1981)
Neapolitan Sting (1982)
Once Upon a Time in America (1984)
Flashpoint (1984)
Smooth Talk (1985)
The Men's Club (1986)
Sweet Lies (1988)
Night of the Sharks (1988)
The Third Solution (1988)
Dead Heat (1988)
Heart of Dixie (1989)

So long Mr. Williams. Thanks for the memories.

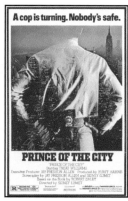

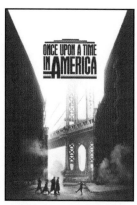

In Memoriam

**Alan Arkin
(1934-2023)**
Actor, known for *Simon* (1980) and *Escape from Sobibor* (1987).

**Jane Birkin
(1946-2023)**
Actress, known for *Evil Under the Sun* (1982) and *Dust* (1985).

**Jim Brown
(1936-2023)**
Actor, known for *The Running Man* (1987) and *I'm Gonna Git You Sucka* (1988).

**William Friedkin
(1935-2023)**
Director, known for *Cruising* (1980) and *To Live and Die in L.A.* (1987).

**Terry Funk
(1944-2023)**
Actor, known for *Over the Top* (1987) and *Road House* (1989).

**Michael Gambon
(1940-2023)**
Actor, known for *The Rachel Papers* (1989) and *The Cook, the Thief, His Wife & Her Lover* (1989).

**Glenda Jackson
(1936-2023)**
Actress, known for *Hopscotch* (1980) and *Salome's Last Dance* (1988).

**Michael Lerner
(1941-2023)**
Actor, known for *Strange Invaders* (1983) and *Vibes* (1988).

**Paul Reubens
(1953-2023)**
Actor, known for *Pee Wee's Big Adventure* (1985) and *Big Top Pee-wee* (1988).

**Tina Turner
(1939-2023)**
Singer and actress, known for *Mad Mad: Beyond Thunderdome* (1985).

"THE STARS ARE THE EYES OF GOD"

TO LIVE AND DIE IN L.A.

by John Harrison

Note: This article contains spoilers.

Having delivered one of the superior crime thrillers of the gritty early '70s in the Oscar-winning *The French Connection* (1971), the late William Friedkin would go on to helm something of a spiritual follow-up, and one of the best neo-noir crime movies of the following decade, in *To Live and Die in L.A.* (1985). Based on the 1984 novel by former United States Secret Service agent Gerald Petievich, who co-wrote the screenplay with Friedkin, the film is not just effective as a galvanizing, hyper-kinetic crime drama, but as a precise and damning encapsulation of '80s Regan America, where excess was both admired and desired, and "Greed is Good" became the mantra, thanks to a sterling speech by Gordon Gekko (Michael Douglas) in Oliver Stone's *Wall Street* (1987).

Richard Chance (William Petersen) and Jimmy Hart (Michael Greene) are United States Secret Service officers, working out of the Los Angeles office while investigating a major counterfeiting operation run by enigmatic artist Eric 'Rick' Masters (Willem Dafoe). In what has since become something of an action film cliché (and a trope often spoofed in comedic send-ups and on shows like *The Simpsons*), Hart is brutally murdered by Masters and his burly bodyguard Jack (Jack Hoar) just three days before he was due to retire. Already an adrenaline junkie with a reckless compulsion, Chance becomes even further driven to nail Masters for the death of his partner and close friend. While his new partner John Vukovich (John Pankow) initially supports Chance in his determination to get Masters "no matter what it takes", he begins to realize that he is being dragged well beyond the call of duty and into a dark, personal obsession that threatens to cost not just his career and his freedom, but potentially his life.

The opening of *To Live and Die in L.A.* comes off almost like Friedkin is doing his own riff on a James Bond adventure, giving us an exciting pre-credit sequence that introduces us to agents Chance and Hart as they stop an Islamic terrorist from bombing President Ronald Regan as he is delivering a speech about taxes to a convention at the Beverly Hilton. As with so many of the 007 pre-credits, this sequence has nothing to do with the main plot of the film. It is there purely to establish the efficiency of the lead character, and the closeness that he has with his partner. There's a surprising tenderness to their partnership, and you can certainly read a bit of interesting gay subtext into their friendship (the way Chance clasps his hand tenderly at the start of the film to reassure him, and later insists that his partner calls him when he gets home, to let him know he is safe, as a concerned wife or mother would usually do).

Just as New York City was as important a character in *The French Connection* as any of the people in it, so too is Los Angeles an integral part of *To Live and Die in L.A.*'s backdrop and drama. But it's not the flashy L.A. of Beverly Hills and posh restaurants, boutique clothing shops and modern malls. Symbolically, while the two main protagonists live in nice surrounds - Chance in an apartment right up against the Malibu beach, and Masters in a spacious white contemporary house in Santa Monica - so much of *To Live and Die in L.A.* takes place in nondescript little bars, nightclub dressing rooms, strip joints, neighborhood hamburger stands and dusty railway yards. One sadly long-gone local landmark that is featured in the film is the infamous Shipyard Joey's strip joint and its distinctive semi-circular entrance and all-white exterior.

Sitting across from the docks of Los Angeles harbour, Shipyard Joey's was demolished not long after it was used as a filming location for *Fight Club* (1999).

One element of the film which makes it feel so authentic is the meticulous way in which Friedkin constructs the scene where Rick Masters, operating out of an old warehouse in the Californian desert, prints up his latest run of counterfeit notes. From the photographing of the plates and the cutting out of the serial numbers, to mixing the ink and printing and cutting the bills, then spinning the notes in the clothes dryer mixed with poker chips to wear off their newness, it is all captured with an almost fetishistic lens by Friedkin and cinematographer Robby Müller. Just like the car accident sequence in *The French Connection* looked straight out of one of those gory driver education shorts made to terrify American high school kids, the counterfeiting scene in *To Live and Die in L.A.* is reminiscent of a classic police training film, where a criminal procedure is explained in detail.

To Live and Die in L.A. provided early notable roles for its three male leads, in particular Petersen and Dafoe.

Petersen, who was working as a stage actor in Chicago at the time, had only one prior film appearance to his name, that being a small role as a bartender in Michael Mann's *Thief* (1981). As the ruthless and reckless anti-hero of the film, Petersen excels at disappearing into a self-destructive character who is charismatic but not very likeable. The actor followed up *To Live and Die in L.A.* with another terrific performance as FBI Agent Will Graham in *Manhunter* (1986), Michael Mann's chilling adaptation of Thomas Harris' novel *Red Dragon*, the book which introduced Dr. Hannibal Lecter to the world. While his film career never really gained the traction it deserved after such a fine start, television success would await Petersen down the track, playing forensic entomologist Gil Grissom on *CSI: Crime Scene Investigation* between 2000 and 2015.

While he had a few more roles to his name than Petersen

did at the time, Dafoe was also still a young actor on the rise when he made *To Live and Die in L.A.* Dafoe's slim build and distinctive facial features - sharp cheekbones, piercing blue eyes, and Joker-esque smile - made him perfect for playing the ruthless, yet tortured and artistically talented Rick Masters. The tensions on display between Petersen and Dafoe during their scenes together is palpable, particularly as their proposed deal to exchange funny money draws closer, and you are left still not sure if Masters is onto the set-up or not. *To Live and Die in L.A.* would mark the beginning of a run of prominent performances by Dafoe, with an Oscar-nominated supporting role in *Platoon* (1986), with *The Last Temptation of Christ* (1988) and *Mississippi Burning* (1988) to come, in a career which remains strong and tremendously varied to this day.

Playing something of a moral compass within the film, Pankow imbues John Vukovich with a perfect level of toughness, uncertainty, and fear. It's the classic conflict that haunts many decent cops - not wanting to go against the unwritten code and rat against his partner, but also wanting to stay true to the values that he swore to uphold when first joining the force. For Vukovich, the pressure feels even more intense, with the added weight of coming from a family that has a tradition in law enforcement excellence. Pankow's filmography is rather limited, with

his work being mostly on stage and in the odd television guest spot.

Aside from the standout lead performances, the supporting cast is also uniformly excellent and typical of Friedkin's impeccable instincts for assembling a powerful ensemble, one which serves the benefit of the film rather than the individual actor. Former child star Dean Stockwell, wonderfully cast here as Masters' confident but conflicted lawyer Bob Grimes, was enjoying something of a career renaissance at the time, thanks to his work on critical arthouse hits like *Paris, Texas* (1984) and *Blue Velvet* (1986), as well as the commercial smash *Beverly Hills Cop II* (1987). Stockwell would cap this period off with a Best Supporting Actor nomination for *Married to the Mob* (1988), before moving back to television to co-star alongside Scott Bakula in the popular science-fiction/fantasy series *Quantum Leap* which ran from 1989 to 1993. It's also great to see the excellent Steve James, a charismatic actor, martial artist, and stunt performer, who plays Jeff, an associate of Masters who gets on his bad side after failing him in a hit job which he had been hired and paid plenty of counterfeit bills for. James became something of a cult figure thanks to his work in lower-budgeted, often direct-to-video action/exploitation fare like *The Exterminator* (1980), *The Delta Force* (1986) and *Hero and the Terror* (1988), as well as *American Ninja* (1985) and its first two sequels. Sadly, he passed away from pancreatic cancer in 1993 at the young age of 41, an unfortunate loss to his many fans and the film world in general.

To Live and Die in L.A. also provided an early notable role for John Turturro, playing the weaselly Carl Cody, who moves paper for Masters until he is captured by Chance and Vudkovich following an exciting foot chase through Los Angeles International Airport. And while the film lacks a traditional female lead, both Debra Feuer and Darlanne Fluegel excel in their supporting roles, Feuer as Bianca Torres, the bi-sexual partner of Masters, Fluegel as Ruth Lanier, a heroin addict on parole whom Chance uses for both sex and information. They both have an ethereal quality about them, along with a vulnerability, and the self-awareness that they are only doing what they need to do to survive, with their looks their most valuable asset. Though Torres has something of a European quality to her, they are both classic L.A. women of the '80s. Fluegel's life would take a tragic turn when she was diagnosed with early-onset Alzheimer's disease at the age of only 56, eventually succumbing to it eight years later in 2017.

Another integral aspect of *To Live and Die in L.A.* is its soundtrack, for which Friedkin boldly eschewed a traditional score and instead brought in English new wave band Wang Chung, who had formed in 1980 and scored a hit single three years later with *Dance Hall Days*. Their score for *To Live and Die in L.A.* comprises of both vocal and instrumental numbers, infused with pounding bass and drums, surrealistic ambient sounds, and supremely catchy pop sensibilities. Friedkin would also direct the music video for the film's title track, which depicts the band in a screening room and editing room, watching the film as they compose and perform the song, which is interspersed with clips from the movie. The soundtrack to the film was released on the Geffen label a couple of months prior to the movie's release, and while the title track climbed to no. 41 on the American Billboard charts, the album itself only managed to make it to no. 85. Still, most soundtracks were not expected to be huge chart hits, so *To Live and Die in L.A.* was successful in that it allowed Wang Chung to be a bit more eclectic and experimental in their sound without the pressure of having to deliver an album of pop hits. It certainly didn't slow down the band's momentum... Wang Chung's next studio album, 1986's *Mosaic*, would spawn two American top ten singles, including their signature tune *Everybody Have Fun Tonight*, which peaked at no. 2 (it was kept off the top spot by The Bangles' *Walk Like an Egyptian*).

It isn't just the soundtrack which helps imbue *To Live and Die in L.A.* with a certain level of flashy MTV slickness.

The film is often edited with the same kind of pace as a music video, which in tandem with the soundtrack helps create an exciting rhythm to the movie. It's also interesting the way in which the occasional onscreen titles that flash up, giving the date and time of the event currently unfolding, uses a different style font each time. The opening title sequence, which follows the pre-credit terrorist scene, also has a very '80s rock video flavour, with a succession of brief shots that not only show us the environs of where the story will unfold, but also manage to effectively convey the way in which counterfeit money is exchanged on the streets, while close-ups of grainy black and white photos and their notations set up the Secret Service investigation angle. Set to the thumping Wang Chung instrumental track *City of the Angels*, and with the title and credits coming up in blood red and bright neon green letters, it provides a perfect example of how to

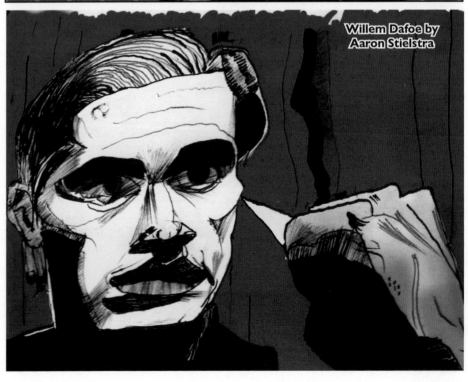

Willem Dafoe by Aaron Stielstra

construct an exciting credit sequence that can artfully do its own thing while also serving the story.

In *To Live and Die in L.A.*, the characters, like the film itself, race ever faster towards their reckoning, in one of the most downbeat and nihilistic endings to ever cap off an '80s action movie, as Chance's recklessness finally catches up to him with the full force of a shotgun blast to the face. Vukovich, physically unharmed but on the verge of complete mental collapse, looks down at his bloodied partner, screaming "You can't do this to me!" at his lifeless body. After he subsequently confronts and kills Masters at his old art warehouse, Vukovich then confronts Ruth, who is hurriedly packing her luggage in order to get the hell out of town, free from Chance's grip but now fearing for her life. Vukovich tells her that she isn't going anywhere… she's working for him now. It gives the film the ugly and morally ambiguous ending which it deserves, and damning comment on how the city, and the life, can transform anyone into a creature of survival.

During production of the film, Friedkin was put under pressure by MGM to deliver something of a more upbeat ending. The studio was concerned that killing off the supposed hero would depress audiences and deter word of mouth and repeat business. Friedkin was adamant that killing Chance was the only logical way for the film to end and make a point. In order to appease the studio,

Friedkin did film an alternate ending, where Chance is only wounded, with the final shot revealing that he and Vukovich have been transferred to a remote station in the cold snow of Anchorage, Alaska. According to Friedkin, he never intended to even consider using the alternate ending, but it worked in that it proved to the MGM execs that the ending originally envisioned by the filmmaker was the correct one. An ending where Chance lived would have robbed the film of much of its impact, and would have lessened the poetic irony of the character's name (the alternate ending can be viewed as a special feature on some of the DVD and Blu-ray releases of the film).

While many people consider the '70s to be Friedkin's best period as a filmmaker, *To Live and Die in L.A.* provides ample proof that he was not just surviving, but thriving, well into the following decade, delivering a vital piece of work which, much like Hitchcock's *Frenzy* (1972), comes off more like it has some audacious and ambitious young hot shot, rather than a seasoned veteran, sitting in the director's chair. Now that Friedkin has left our world, movies like *To Live and Die in L.A.* become something even more important to embrace and cherish… unique masterworks from a unique artist, movies that don't pull their punches, just as the filmmaker himself was never afraid to speak his own mind.

"They Kill to Survive"
WOLFEN

by Michael Campochiaro

"*In arrogance man knows nothing of what exists. There exists on this earth such as we dare not imagine; life as certain as our death, life that will prey on us as surely as we prey on this earth.*"

If 1981 was the Year of the Werewolf in cinemas, where does Michael Wadleigh's odd and disarming *Wolfen* fit in that mix? Unlike the two most popular and lasting werewolf films of 1981, *The Howling* and *An American Werewolf in London*, *Wolfen* is not really a werewolf film but instead an indictment on America's historic, horrific mistreatment of its indigenous peoples and the modern-day mistreatment of its inner cities. Urban decay is placed front and center. Colonizers stole the land out from under the Native Americans' feet, then relegated them to the shadows of society while simultaneously laying waste to large swaths of this land. Filmed in New York City during the height of the city's "Bronx is Burning" era, *Wolfen* makes

extraordinary use of the Bronx's blown-out buildings and brick mountains of rubble. The film serves as a potent reminder of just how callously inner-city residents were treated at that time, left to suffer and fend for themselves by a society that didn't care about them - because of the color of their skin, and their economic and class status. Politics and greed drove decision-making, while the human factor was largely ignored. Sounds familiar, doesn't it? We haven't learned much in the decades since *Wolfen's* release.

Let's backtrack for a moment to delve into the film's plot, then tackle some of its core themes. Based on Whitley Strieber's 1978 horror novel 'The Wolfen', Wadleigh's film offers a very loose adaptation that makes substantial changes to the novel, wiping out entire portions while shifting focus to issues barely even hinted at in the book. Strieber tells the story of a pack of predators hunting and preying on New Yorkers. The police are stymied, as

10

the grisly murders seem to be the work of an advanced humanoid beast. As unbelievable as it sounds to the novel's very rational characters, this turns out to be the truth. The two main investigating police detectives soon find themselves the targets of these supernatural predators. The Wolfen, as they are dubbed in the novel, are an ancient species that has evolved into a superior, dominant race of hunters. Driven to the shadows of our forests and cities, the Wolfen live among us, creeping and stalking before striking when the need for feeding arises. They seek to protect themselves and their kin from the horrors of man's world. The novel is extremely gory and graphic in its depictions of these murders, and the Wolfen themselves are terrifying. They are very clearly depicted as supernatural werewolf-like beasts with powers and abilities far beyond normal wolves.

The screenplay, by David M. Eyre, Jr., Wadleigh, and an uncredited assist from Eric Roth, dispenses with the werewolf form of the Wolfen, instead using actual wolves. The supernatural element remains intact though, but in the film the predators themselves are basically superpowered, highly evolved wolves with heightened abilities. For much of the film, they are kept offscreen or in shadows. We don't see them often, until the final act. In the novel, Strieber takes us inside the minds of the Wolfen, exploring their inner thoughts and emotions in great detail. Some of the book is even told from their perspective. Wadleigh and cinematographer Gerry Fisher (*The Exorcist III*) devised a brilliant visual way to translate this to the screen,

pioneering an in-camera effect like thermography that shows us the wolves' subjective point of view as they stalk the city for their prey. This technique would later be popularized thanks to its use in *Predator*, but *Wolfen* did it first and did it beautifully. The way Wadleigh quickly cuts to these POV shots is always jarring, enhancing the sense of terror. The POV shots remind us that, although man believes this to be his world, the Wolfen see it otherwise.

Wolfen adds in several elements that are not present in Strieber's novel, including most prominently themes related to Native Americans. The indigenous characters in the film work on New York City's large suspension bridges, serving as the police investigator's source for information regarding the Wolfen. The Native characters, along with South Bronx New Yorkers and the Wolfen themselves, are all being pushed to the margins by man's unending march towards "progress," which is really code for "conquest." The film doesn't sugarcoat any of this, and even though

WOLFEN

WOLFEN

WOLFEN

WOLFEN

WOLFEN

we're aligned with two white heroes - the detectives working the murders - we are continually reminded of how their ancestors stole away land that didn't even belong to them. The plight of the film's indigenous peoples, the South Bronx residents and the Wolfen all serve as constant reminders of man's seemingly unlimited propensity for cruelty.

One element of the book that the film captures well is a strong sense of place. Strieber's detailed descriptions of various nooks and corners of the city is brought to rich, visual life by Wadleigh. Few films from the period deliver as strong a sense of place as Wolfen. The city lives and breathes, acting as a vital supporting character in the narrative. From the opening shot of buildings being demolished in the South Bronx as the title card appears onscreen to harrowing scenes filmed atop the Manhattan Bridge, *Wolfen* follows it predators and police investigators as they traverse the city. The bridge scene must be seen to be believed, in fact, as it appears the camera crew and actors (Albert Finney and Edward James Olmos) were indeed perched precariously atop the suspension bridge. Stunning location work in Central Park, Battery Park, Coney Island, Wall Street and Riverside Drive give the film a sense of time and place that today acts as an essential document of that difficult time in America, and specifically in New York City.

The city provides much of the film's atmosphere, but Wadleigh and crew masterfully build their own horror-style atmospherics as well. Nearly every moment is filled with a pervasive, looming sense of dread. Much of the action is filmed at night on the city's streets, or in shadow-draped modernist apartments and ornate office buildings, with

Albert Finney by
Aaron Stielstra

characters trying to make sense of the savage attacks plaguing the city. Rarely mentioned in the same breath as other horror classics, *Wolfen's* horror credentials remain unimpeachable to me. Every moment works towards the ultimate goal of keeping viewers on edge, off balance, and at times frightened of what might be coming next. The cast deserves a tremendous amount of credit for handling the material with an earnestness that makes it all seem entirely believable. Albert Finney is exceptional as Detective Dewey Wilson. After several years away

from cinemas, during which time he worked exclusively onstage, Finney returned with lead roles in three 1981 films - *Loophole*, *Wolfen* and *Looker*. In *Wolfen*, he creates a unique character who wears rumpled clothes, sports permanently tousled bedhead hair, and scoffs down doughnuts after a jog. Dewey Wilson is a different sort of cop: a mesmerizingly eccentric one. In an early scene, after Dewey has been called in to the first crime scene, he carries around the brown bag of groceries he had just purchased at the corner store. It's hilarious to watch him discussing the gruesome details of the murder with a city coroner (a fantastic Gregory Hines) as they look over the dead bodies. Most crucially though, this detail adds a key character note that tells us more about Dewey than any amount of exposition could: he's dedicated to his work, and extremely pragmatic. Why stop quickly at home to drop off the groceries when you can just carry them around the crime scene and munch on doughnuts at the same time? In a career full of excellent performances, *Wolfen* might be my favorite of Finney's roles. Future versions of the Dewey character - the eccentric loner, obsessed with their job to the point of not caring about things like social graces and manners - would become a Hollywood cliché, but in Finney's hands it's a deftly crafted character who feels fully realized in every way.

Diane Venora gets second billing in her first film role, as Detective Rebecca Neff, a criminal psychologist assigned to be Wilson's partner on the case. In the novel, Neff is as central a character to the story as her partner (named George Wilson in the book). Together, she and Wilson have a fascinating older cop-younger cop relationship that builds from snarky banter into mutual love and respect as they work the case and try to protect each other from becoming the Wolfen's next victims. The film makes attempts at building a romance between Neff and Wilson, but much of the work that went into this in the novel is jettisoned for the film. Venora doesn't have as much to

13

do as Finney, which is a shame because she's extremely talented and has good chemistry with her co-star. Even if the script didn't give her as much material to work with as I'd have liked, she still manages to make Neff into an interesting character. Her big, expressive eyes do a lot of the heavy lifting and she's a pleasure to watch alongside Finney.

The supporting cast is full of wonderful character actors, and each makes a big impression. There's Hines as the charismatic coroner Whittington. The younger, funnier foil for Finney's grouchy middle-aged Dewey, Hines radiates charisma whenever he's onscreen. Tom Noonan plays an endearing, oddball zoologist named Ferguson. Dick

O'Neill is entertaining as the gruff and sarcastic police Captain Warren. Edward James Olmos plays the fierce Native activist and convicted criminal Eddie Holt, in a performance that's positively electrifying. Any time Olmos appears, the tension and energy levels skyrocket. Eddie's ominous intonations about Native American spirituality and shapeshifting lore add further layers of mystery and intrigue to the film. Eddie and other indigenous characters know more about the Wolfen - "the wolf spirit" - than anyone else in the film. They speak of them in hushed whispers, noting that these extraordinary creatures might even be gods. *Wolfen* is the sort of film that grows on me with each additional viewing. I've watched it several times, including again for this piece, and every time I find more reasons to adore it. The atmospherics, the acting, the social commentary and the mystical and supernatural elements combine to make a film that's tough to categorize but exciting to watch. While it deviates greatly from the terrific source material - Strieber's 'The Wolfen' is an addictively readable, taut exercise in horror fiction - *Wolfen* doesn't suffer by comparison for it. Instead, the film is full of themes and issues that only further accentuate and enhance its horror elements. *Wolfen* is truly scary at times, no question about it. The Wolfen POV shots create a tense and suffocating sense of impending doom every time they're deployed. The scene inside a decaying Bronx building, when the Wolfen nearly kill Neff before Finney saves her life, is framed and sequenced beautifully, ratcheting up the tension levels with every shot.

All these years later, *Wolfen* remains a bit of an anomaly in the werewolf cinematic canon. It probably shouldn't even be lumped into the werewolf category at all, but it's a useful shorthand for people to know that the film involves wolves with extraordinary abilities and instincts that are fighting to protect what once belonged to them. *Wolfen* deals frankly and forthrightly with difficult issues, while also being a thoroughly entertaining film. Wadleigh displayed a knack for horror directing, and it's a terrible shame he never directed another movie again. Still, he left us with the enigmatic, thoughtful and atmospheric *Wolfen*, a title worthy of being considered among the best New York City films of its time and among the best horror movies of 1981.

by Simon J. Ballard

"The Salkinds decided to make an epic in two parts... I don't know what got them to take that decision" - *Superman* co-writer Robert Benton.

The Salkinds (Polish-born father and son Alexander and Ilya), along with French producer Pierre Spengler, bought the rights to the D.C. Comics hero Superman in 1974, soon after making the swashbuckling romps *The Three* and *Four Musketeers* in 1973. The back-to-back approach they'd used on the *Musketeers* project worked quite well, so they saw no reason why director Richard Donner couldn't do the same with *Superman*. The postman nearly had a hernia when he delivered the gargantuan scripts for Part I and II! These had been written from a story by 'The Godfather' author Mario Puzo, who left after working on the first two drafts and was replaced by David and Leslie Newman and Benton.

Martin Dallard covered the making of *Superman* (1978) in Issue 3 of our sister publication 'Cinema of the '70s'. Here, I'll be focusing on the '80s entries: *Superman II*, *Superman III* and *Superman IV: The Quest for Peace*.

Having helmed the blockbuster *The Omen* (1976), Donner was experienced in the art of realising a big-budget movie on a lengthy schedule. Nevertheless, *Superman* put him under considerable pressure from the start. "I don't think they [the Salkinds and Spengler] had any concept what the film would be... their sole interest was: 'How do we make it cheaper?'" he remarked.

Donner kept his bubbling frustrations to himself as he busied himself with the task at hand. Since he was making two movies simultaneously, he planned to shoot all the footage based in a specific set or location in one go, irrespective of whether it would be used in Part I or II. Story-wise, the original climax to *Superman* was supposed to see Superman flinging one of Lex Luther's nuclear missiles into space, accidentally releasing Kryptonian rebels Zod, Ursa and Non from their eternal imprisonment in

The Phantom Zone, leading nicely into the sequel. But the antipathy between Donner and the producers just wouldn't go away, so much so that the director couldn't talk to them nor even stand the sight of them.

Ilya came up with the idea of hiring their *Musketeers* director Richard Lester for "an undefined position" on the big-budget picture. Ostensibly recruited as a line producer, the reality was that Lester was brought in to liaise between Donner and the producers. He mainly took the job because they still owed him for the two *Musketeers* pictures! Thankfully, Lester and Donner were friends so the situation was made easier, but the threat of being fired loomed over Donner's head throughout. Margot Kidder, who played Lois Lane, would later marvel at how well he hid his prickly predicament from the cast.

In such a precarious position, Donner decided to park Part II and concentrate all his efforts on Part I. By this point, 70% of the footage for Part II had already been shot. Journalist Army Archerd described the on-set tensions in 'Variety' after speaking to Donner about his feelings towards Spengler and his thoughts on the sequel. "If he [Spengler] is in on it - I'm out!" Donner declared, saying he could just about take the Salkinds but describing Spengler as intolerable.

Spengler was a good friend of the Salkinds, so it was no surprise when shortly afterwards Donner received a telegram bluntly stating: 'Your services will no longer be needed.' This was a crushing blow, making him feel like his baby had been taken away. At least he could console himself with the huge success of Part I when it hit the screens, wowing audiences around the world.

Lester was tasked with filming the remaining sequences for Part II. Now, in the movie business, a director must shoot at least 40% of a picture to be officially credited as director so when Donner refused a joint credit, it became clear large portions of the sequel would need to be reshot in order to put Lester's name on it. Known for his economical filmmaking, Lester decided it would be too expensive to retain the footage of Marlon Brando as Jor-El in Part II, so his lines were given to Susannah York as Lara (Superman's mother) and John Hollis as a Krypton elder. York's inclusion brings a nice emotional balance to the saga, after the fatherly sage advice espoused in Part I.

Gene Hackman, playing villain Lex Luthor, was fiercely loyal to Donner and refused to play any part in Lester's reshoots (all scenes in *Superman II* which feature Hackman were shot by Donner). In the Fortress of Solitude after Lex Luthor's prison break, for example, Hackman is really reacting to Brando's unused offstage material.

So, what in *Superman II* is Donner and what is Lester? Hold on tight! The movie begins with the arrest of the supervillains on Krypton, a voiceover replacing Brando's presence. After their imprisonment, the credits flash through a recap of the previous entry, and even here some tinkering was needed (e.g a close-up of Brando's hand had to be removed).

The film proper begins with newspaper boss Perry White (Jackie Cooper) announcing to Clark Kent and photographer Jimmy Olsen (Marc McClure) that Lois is covering a terrorist threat in Paris, leading to Kent changing into Superman in a back alley and zooming off to France. This subplot was not a feature of Donner's version, which began with Lois leaping out of White's office window to prove Kent and Superman are one and the same.

The terrorists are ensconced in an elevator up the Eiffel Tower, with Lois eavesdropping from its underside. Viewers who suffer from vertigo may feel a little queasy at the sight of her clinging on as the lift ascends to ever greater heights, even more so when the terrorists' hydrogen bomb (that's one way to make your demands felt) is accidentally detonated. All this is pure Lester, culminating in a sequence where Superman carries the elevator into outer space so it can be blown up without causing death or damage. Shockwaves from the resulting explosion inadvertently release the supervillains Zod, Ursa and Non.

Signs of Lester's lighter touch are felt in a subsequent scene as Clark crosses a busy road only for a yellow cab to bump into him, smashing its radiator to pieces. Even better is the sight of Lois freshly squeezing oranges with a cigarette in her mouth.

The prison scenes featuring Hackman and Ned Beatty (as dim-witted sidekick Otis) are Donner, of course, all leading up to their escape aided by plucky secretary Miss Teschmacher (played with infectious charm by Valerie Perrine). We continue with the Donner footage with scenes of astronauts taking soil samples on the surface of the moon. There's a neat satirical stab at how such landings were being perceived as just another humdrum activity - "More rocks, thanks," grumbles Shane Rimmer's bored Houston technician. As Zod, Ursa, and Non land, they attack the moon-rakers and destroy the landing craft in a visually stunning set-piece that no doubt was thought too costly to remount. The moon set is very impressive - it wouldn't surprise me if it spurred a few conspiracy loonies to comment how easy it must have been to fake the 1969 moon landings!

A mention must be made here of our nasty trio from Krypton. Terence Stamp oozes malevolence and contempt as Zod, while Sarah Douglas brings a sadistic edge to Ursa who is in thrall of her master yet revels in the suffering of others. She rips the NASA badge off an astronaut, killing him in the vacuum of space, which in turn instigates a recurring sight gag throughout in which her black costume ends up adorned with trophies from her victims - a CCCP emblem, a sheriff's badge and an American general's ribbons! Rounding off the trio is Jack O'Halloran as Nod, offering a mute performance as a child-like giant excited by his newfound powers. He just wants to make his master happy, like some superhuman puppy. He kills, yet he's oddly sweet!

Lester is responsible for the sequence in which Clark and Lois visit Niagara Falls to investigate fraud in the leisure industry. In the theatrical (e.g. Lester) version, Lois tests her suspicion that Kent is Superman by throwing herself into the treacherous waters. Combining shots of Kidder on a hidden platform, a stunt performer doing the more dangerous stuff, and some close-up shots in the water tank at Pinewood Studies, this sequence is very

well done. Superman firmly refuses to reveal himself, with Clark feigning panic from the sidelines while Lois is tossed through the raging rapids!

The revelation does occur, however, a little later when Clark trips and manages not to burn his hands in the hotel room fire. Lois' statement that she is in love with Superman was not to everyone's liking, but personally I have no problem with it. The emotional heart behind Part I was down to Superman's journey of self-discovery, helped along by recorded words of wisdom from his father. We also, of course, had the romantic scene where he takes Lois on a nighttime flight. It made sense to develop their burgeoning romance in this sequel, and when Superman renounces his special powers so he can live as a mortal with Lois, there's a wonderful irony in the awfulness of his timing, losing his superhuman abilities just as Zod and co. arrive to terrorise the world. When Zod lands in a river then walks on the surface, there is a dark parallel with the allusions to Christ in Superman's back story.

Another element in the emotional development of Superman and Lois comes from how he sees himself. Until the age of eighteen, he thought he was Clark Kent of Smallville, so we're left wondering if Clark remains in his mind when he's Superman? It's telling in an earlier scene how put out Clark is when Lois says she perceives him as just a friend. When he enters the molecule chamber and allows himself to be stripped of his powers, does he feel more like the self he grew up believing himself to be? Does he feel happier, relieved of a great burden?

Reeve and Kidder gel extremely well, building on the chemistry they'd formed in the initial entry, and it is a

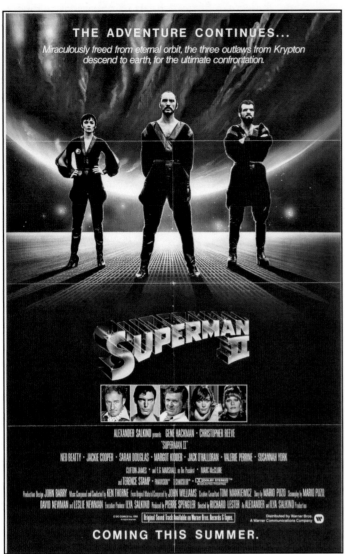

testament to them that they give strong performances despite the trying circumstances behind the scenes. Lester was a very different director to Donner, shooting almost in the manner of a television production with three cameras trained on the action at the same time. The performers didn't always know when they were in close-ups and distance shots, but any measure of uncertainly never comes across on screen.

Of note is the cruel juxtaposition of Superman and Lois' burgeoning romance and scenes of the supervillains attacking a Midwest town. The Lester-shot devastation looks effective thanks to Derek Meddings' superlative model effects, including a military helicopter being blown off course by Ursa's breath and crashing into a barn. Neither flame-throwers nor missile launchers cause much damage to the Kryptonian villains. "Is there no-one on this planet to even challenge me?" Zod roars.

Well, having had a word with his mum via several million light years, it's not going to be the newly mortal, mild-mannered Clark Kent, that's for sure! While Clark adjusts to life without superpowers, the villains deface Mount Rushmore (replacing the carved images of past presidents with their own) and attack the White House. What we are seeing here, as soldiers are swatted away like flies, is footage shot by Donner (apart from a couple of close pick-up shots, including an American flag falling forlornly to the ground). Stamp is coldly amusing when the President bows down before him and bleakly mutters "Oh God", to which he corrects: "Zod."

There's more Donner footage as Lois and Clark enter a diner. In fact, as the car approaches, Donner makes a

cameo, strolling past on the left as they approach. Ilya Salkind used this as an example of how Donner had mellowed towards the producers, but he was quick to point out that he allowed the cameo to remain so that audiences would eventually come to know that the diner scene - as Clark is viciously beaten up - was down to him. It is a rather stark moment as the former Man of Steel contemplates the sight of his blood for the first time, displaying some of that emotive edge Donner brought to Part I. Also noticeable here - as in several other Donner-shot scenes - is the difference in hair length between Reeve and Kidder.

Stamp's hair also shortens from one shot to the next in the scene where Luthor pays the villains a visit in the White House, offering to introduce them to the son of Jor-El in return for being allowed to call himself ruler of Australia! Whilst these negotiations take place, Clark returns to his Fortress, which is even more desolate and dark since he surrendered his super-status, but the hardy green crystal which called him to the spot in the first place still glows with hope.

With close-ups shot by Lester, we see Lois feeling hopeless back at the Daily Planet, realising her chance of happiness has been dashed by the arrival of the three Kryptonian villains. She is never less than compellingly watchable, but her facial expressions and terse delivery really make you feel her pain. We're back with Donner footage as the villains burst through the newspaper office, creating havoc in their wake as they fail to use one single doorknob, Luthor in tow. Again, look out for Kidder's hair and make-up which changes alarmingly between shots depending on who directed what.

The ensuing battle for Metropolis, with the returned Superman ordering the supervillains to step outside, is all down to Lester. Combining a life-size replica of Manhattan (doubling for the fictional 'Metropolis'), back projection and miniature models at Pinewood, this is a stunning sequence. The four wage an extraordinary battle using flag poles, drain covers, a bus tossed in the air - both real and model - as well as their own superpowers of laser eyes and extreme blowing of wind (stop sniggering). There is some rather obvious product placement as Superman is pushed by the skidding bus into a Marlboro van, somewhat counteracting a poster campaign featuring Superman revealing the effect of smoking on lungs via his x-ray vision! There is also a moment in which Zod is flung into a gigantic neon Coca-Cola sign.

How can you tell Lester helmed these scenes? It's the humorous touches, like Zod's wind (stop it, I tell you!) blowing a man's wig off and causing another man to pirouette with an umbrella, Gene Kelly-style, and a man at a phone booth carrying on with his conversation despite being knocked to the ground.

THE ADVENTURE CONTINUES

The three outlaws from Krypton descend to Earth to confront the Man of Steel, in a cosmic battle for world supremacy.

SUPERMAN II

ALEXANDER SALKIND presents GENE HACKMAN · CHRISTOPHER REEVE
"SUPERMAN II"
NED BEATTY · JACKIE COOPER · SARAH DOUGLAS
MARGOT KIDDER · JACK O'HALLORAN · VALERIE PERRINE · SUSANNAH YORK CLIFTON JAMES and E.G. MARSHALL as the President · MARC McCLURE
and TERENCE STAMP PANAVISION® TECHNICOLOR® DOLBY STEREO™ IN SELECTED THEATRES

Production Design JOHN BARRY Music Composed and Conducted by KEN THORNE From Original Material Composed by JOHN WILLIAMS Creative Consultant TOM MANKIEWICZ Story by MARIO PUZO Screenplay by MARIO PUZO,
DAVID NEWMAN and LESLIE NEWMAN Executive Producer ILYA SALKIND Produced by PIERRE SPENGLER Directed by RICHARD LESTER An ALEXANDER and ILYA SALKIND Production

PG PARENTAL GUIDANCE SUGGESTED
SOME MATERIAL MAY NOT BE SUITABLE FOR CHILDREN
© DC COMICS Inc. 1981
All Rights Reserved
Original Sound Track Available on Warner Bros. Records & Tapes.
Distributed by Warner Bros.
A Warner Communications Company

This humour was more to the Salkinds' liking, the kind of thing Donner was keen to stamp out, and which Lester would emphasise even more with Part III.

Bar some Lester close-ups and shots of a double playing Luthor from behind, it's all Donner for the final showdown at the Fortress of Solitude. Superman cunningly reverses the molecule chamber's power, so that while he is safe inside, the villains outside are drained of their power. These scenes are a mess, frankly. As Non looms over him, Superman plucks a plasticky 'S' from his chest which envelops the brute, and at one-point multiple versions of Superman appear at once. Not sure what's going on here!

Donner also provides the satisfying payoff as Clark gets his revenge on the guy at the diner, maintaining his mild-mannered persona throughout. But it's Lester who's behind the heroic final call as Superman returns the flag to prominence atop the ruinous White House, declaring never to let down the nation again.

So, with portions of Donner's 1977 footage combined with Lester's newly shot '79 material, was *Superman II* able to score big at the box office? The short answer is 'yes'. Naturally, the tone is uneven and, as I've said, a few continuity mishaps jar slightly, but overall it is a hugely enjoyable sequel that flows at a good pace. Apart from some awful sight gags, it builds on the epic scale and wit of the previous entry. A Richard Donner cut was released in 2006 in collaboration with the director, but it's a curio at best. Ironically, it still utilises some Lester footage to tell the tale the way Donner intended to present it.

And so onto the next instalment. "Eulogies are certainly in order for *Superman III*," a critic wrote, "a pale and pathetic third entry."

Harsh words for the second sequel which, totally free from Donner's solemn influence, builds on the comedic aspects of the previous entry. Ilya initially proposed a treatment for Part III that drew its influences straight from the comic, with Superman teaming up with his cousin Supergirl to defeat a villain named Brainiac and his mischief-making partner Mr Mxyzptlk from the Fifth Dimension! Warner Bros took one look at this proposal and shook their heads vigorously.

Richard Pryor may have been a comedian, but he was only joking on *The Tonight Show* when he told Johnny Carson he'd love to be in *Superman*. Ilya, however, took his words literally and told David and Leslie Newman to fashion a script for *Superman III* which would feature a prominent part for Pryor. Thus was born Gus Gorman, a gormless bum and computer genius whose talents are sought by industrialist Ross Webster (Robert Vaughn), the head of Webscoe, who

wishes to take control of the coffee and oil industries of the world. Webster is joined in his dastardly plan by sister Vera (played with acidic venom by Annie Ross) and his supposedly ditsy airhead of a girlfriend Lorelei (the bubbly and effervescent Pamela Stephenson). I love the way Lorelei is secretly a well-read intellectual (reading Kant at

one point).

One new character transferred from comic to screen is Lana Lang, a high school crush from Clark's Smallville years, whose son Ricky idolises the superhero. Annette O'Toole adds a great deal of fresh-faced charm in the role. There are two theories about Lana's prominence in Part III. Margot Kidder's vociferous support for Donner might have caused her to be sidelined for this entry (Lois heads to Bermuda to cover a story, and is seen only at the beginning and end of the movie). But Ilya claimed that once Superman had kissed Lois and revealed the secret of his dual identity to her, their story had run its course and therefore a new love interest was needed.

Superman III is a pure Lester movie, and boy do we know it! The titles play out to some rather tedious physical gags, involving phone booths collapsing, pratfalls, and a custard pie in the face before an armed robbery leads to Superman saving a man trapped in his car after changing in a photo booth. In a rather sweet touch, the little boy Superman hands his photo to is played by Aaron Smolinski (who'd played baby Clark in Part I).

I must admit that, as a Pryor fan, I rather love his presence throughout Part III. The man himself, though,

was unhappy at being saddled with such a goofy role, hoping he'd get to flex the seriocomic acting muscles he'd demonstrated in *Silver Streak* and *Stir Crazy*.

A fire at a chemical plant showcases some excellent practical effects, with a neat payoff in which the superhero puts it out by freezing an entire lake and dropping it on the plant. Later he attends a high school reunion in Smallville in which he catches up with Lana Lang. The slightly stuttered romance here is played nicely, and again we get the notion that Superman feels truer to himself when he's in Clark's shoes. He certainly more than enjoys the company of Lana.

The main plot incorporates more daft comedy, as a drunken Gus infiltrates the mainframe computer of Webscoe causing a satellite to create a storm over Colombia, ruining the country's entire coffee crop - an act of petulance on Webster's part. As he fiddles the system, a traffic system breaks down, causing the red and green men of a pedestrian crossing to engage in a fight (it's the Superman equivalent of the double-taking pigeon from *Moonraker*).

If the world's most powerful computer can control even Superman...no one on earth is safe!

SUPERMAN III

ALEXANDER SALKIND presents
CHRISTOPHER REEVE · RICHARD PRYOR
in "SUPERMAN III"

JACKIE COOPER · MARC McCLURE · ANNETTE O'TOOLE · ANNIE ROSS
PAMELA STEPHENSON · ROBERT VAUGHN and MARGOT KIDDER as Lois Lane
Music by KEN THORNE · Theme by GIORGIO MORODER · Story by DAVID and LESLIE NEWMAN · Executive Producer ILYA SALKIND
Produced by PIERRE SPENGLER · Written by RICHARD LESTER · Directed by ALEXANDER and ILYA SALKIND
RELEASED BY WARNER BROS.
A WARNER COMMUNICATIONS COMPANY

make *Superman IV: The Quest for Peace* and all I can say at this point is "Come back, Part III... all is forgiven!"

"We wanted to bring something new and fresh to *Superman*," Yoram proclaimed in a retrospective interview. What they delivered was a cut-price movie (the budget was slashed at the eleventh hour from $36 million to $17 million) and a trite storyline, co-provided by Reeve, in which Superman promises to rid the world of nuclear weapons. The epic scale of the Salkinds' vision is downgraded to such an extent that a bus station in Milton Keynes stands in for the UN building, with a fire hydrant stuck in the middle of the shot to add some American 'authenticity'! Heck, the credits include special thanks to C&A and Didcot Power Station!

Veteran director Sidney J. Furie tries hard with the paucity of money and invention, but he faces an uphill and

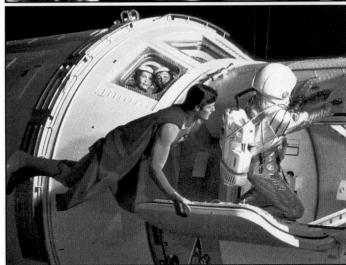

Before I get too negative, special mention must be made of Reeve's barnstorming performance when he is handed tar-infused Kryptonite by Gus which turns him bad. The sight of ol' Supes drunk in a bar, flicking nuts and smashing bottles, gave me chills as a kid, and the fight in the scrapyard between Evil Superman and Good Superman is stunning to watch. Pat Roach of *Indiana Jones* and *Auf Wiedersehen, Pet* fame doubled as Bad Superman in certain shots, in a sequence that was filmed on the backlot at Pinewood. In the background, sharp-eyed viewers will spot the 007 stage (in which Gus' supercomputer set was installed).

After the epic nature of Part I, and the supervillain battles of Part II, a lighter approach for Part III wasn't a bad idea in principle, but Lester encourages Pryor to mug too much and Vaughn's Webster is too urbane to offer any counteracting menace. The sight of his sister being turned into a cyborg by the supercomputer's defences is also rather silly. *Superman III* is fun in places, but ultimately the whole is rather lacklustre. Plans for Part IV were put on hold by Ilya's desire to make *Supergirl*.

The Salkinds and Spengler left the franchise at this point. Enter Israeli cousins Menahem Golan and Yoram Globus of Cannon Films. They snapped up the rights to ultimately unwinnable struggle. Screenwriters Lawrence Kanner and Mark Rosenthal recycle material, such as Superman and Lois flying together (Zoran Perisic's groundbreaking lenses from the previous entries is substituted with some awful matting) along with the memory-wiping kiss from Part II. The green crystal restores Superman's powers again, and Lex contacts Superman via ultrasonics once more.

Mark Pillow camps it up something rotten as the villainous Nuclear Man, complete with extendable silver nails, though it's lovely to have Hackman back. His scenes are some of the best in the movie, though he is compromised

somewhat by the presence of Jon Cryer as his inane, irritating nephew Lenny who, after springing him from jail, serves no purpose whatsoever.

Despite cutting back on the money, Part IV does boast some rather nice model work. My favourite is the volcano Nuclear Man causes to erupt (Superman cuts the top off a nearby mountain and corks it!) Kidder is given greater prominence than in Part III and the battle scenes are fun - check out the creases in the backcloth on those moon surface scenes - and Mariel Hemingway plays the part of spoilt but conscience-ridden Lacy, daughter of tycoon David Warfield, nicely. But what in the name of sanity were they thinking during the scene where Lacy is kidnapped by Nuclear Man and flown out into deep space?! She's still breathing! How?!?! Why?!?!

Part IV brought an ignominious end to Reeve's run as frankly the greatest Superman there has been. He hated it, giving it only a one-sentence mention in his memoirs, and so too did audiences. The box office takings were by far the lowest in the series.

The law of diminishing returns eventually proved as devastating to the sequels as a lump of Kryptonite. But without *Superman* and its sequels, we would not have the run of Batman or Spiderman features - and all the rest - we have now. *Superman* and its sequels proved for the first time that a superhero franchise could fly!

HEARTBREAK RIDGE

Surviving an '80s Slump and Other Battles

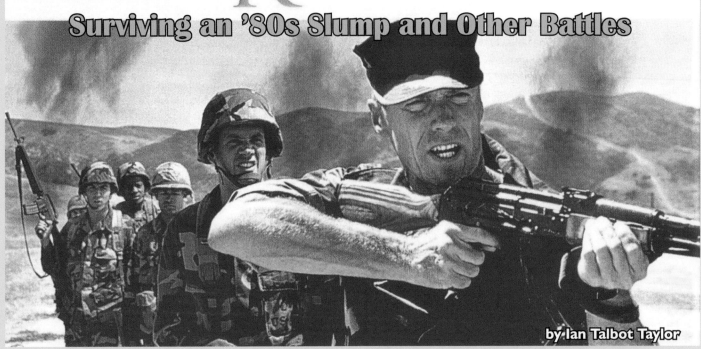

by Ian Talbot Taylor

There aren't many Clint Eastwood war films, are there? His career has been made up predominantly of westerns and thrillers. The wartime set exceptions are small pre-fame roles in *Away All Boats* (1956) and *Lafayette Escadrille* (1958) followed by *Where Eagles Dare* (1968), *Kelly's Heroes* (1970) and *Firefox* (1982). He also directed the latter and would find himself drawn to helming true-life tales of conflict with *Flags of Our Fathers, Letters from Iwo Jima* (both 2006) and *American Sniper* (2014).

The one other war film on Eastwood's list of credits is *Heartbreak Ridge* which was released in the US and Australia in December 1986 and in the UK in January 1987. This was yet another project combining Eastwood's skills as both actor and director, something which had become the norm, with him only being directed by someone else four times between *The Outlaw Josey Wales* in 1976 and *Heartbreak Ridge* 10 years later, whilst he took control himself on nine productions. One always got the feeling that directing was what interested Eastwood most, and he was willing to do so on any number of pictures, not just his personal passion projects, in order to attain the high levels he strove for. Likewise, he would occasionally take on acting roles simply to help grease the wheels of the stuff that he was really interested in doing. There is surely no other way to explain the existence of Clint movies such as *The Dead Pool* (1988), *Pink Cadillac* (1989) and *The*

Rookie (1990), all of which star the great man (who also directs the last). These all offer him roles that could have been just as easily played by any number of '80s action stars, including those of the bargain bucket, straight-to-video standard.

In short, Eastwood was at a transitional point in his career. There, in the '80s, he was standing at a crossroads whereby the decisions he made might lead along a road to the final career act of increasingly disappointing vehicles boasting relentlessly decreasing budgets and ratings. We all know that road; it's the one taken, for one reason or another, by the likes of Charles Bronson, Chuck Norris and many more. Of course, Eastwood being the thoughtful practitioner that he was (and remains), opted to take the other route, sucking up those late '80s projects and using the material benefits of them to pave the way for movies such as *White Hunter, Black Heart* (1990), which was nominated for the Palme d'Or Award at the Cannes Film Festival and *Unforgiven* (1992), the film that won him Best Picture and Best Director Awards at the Oscars, as well as a Best Actor nomination.

Heartbreak Ridge lands at a significantly pivotal point in time. 1984 saw the crushing disappointment of *City Heat*, the movie that promised so much with its teaming up of Eastwood and Burt Reynolds but performed badly at the box office and did neither career much good. Ill-served

by the directing of Richard Benjamin and the writing of Blake Edwards, Clint had to fall back on a stereotypical Eastwood performance, and too much of that is what can easily lead to diminishing quality and returns and the straight-to-video releases of multiple sequels. He regained ground the following year with the gorgeous looking and enjoyable *Pale Rider*, but there was no escaping the fact that the picture rehashed elements of Eastwood's own *High Plains Drifter* (1972) and Jack Shaefer's classic novel 'Shane'. Again, this was more of the Clint Eastwood of expectations.

Heartbreak Ridge at least rang the changes by opting for the more atypical army setting (though reflective tales of contemporary uniformed conflict and their after-effects were becoming *de rigueur* thanks to the likes of Michael Cimino's *The Deer Hunter* (1978), Francis Ford Coppola's *Apocalypse Now* (1979), Stallone in *First Blood* (1982), Hackman in *Uncommon Valor* (1983) and Oliver Stone's *Platoon* (1986) and Stanley Kubrick's *Full Metal Jacket* (1987) which, despite both being released after *Heartbreak Ridge*, had begun the filmmaking process before it. Soon, many name actors and directors would have something comparable on their credit list. Eastwood might as well have joined in.

In its favour, *Heartbreak Ridge* allowed the actor to present himself as older, and in some ways more fragile and flawed, a precursor of such projects as *Unforgiven* and *In the Line of Fire* (1993) and, let's face it, most of his career thereafter. This lack of vanity and deeper consideration of more complex aspects of character and situation would become one of Eastwood's strengths, as opposed to the repetitive cycle that such as Charles Bronson would become trapped in.

At the same time, Clint's character of Gunnery Sergeant Thomas Highway is a knowing creation that borders on caricature but celebrates the fact. This is a typical Eastwood portrayal turned up to the max, with more one-liners, comic squints, glares and grimaces and hard-nosed bits of action to please the more gung-ho fans, but beneath it all there is something more complex going on. It borders on meta as this celebrated star presents an exaggerated version of his most popular portrayals used for comic as well as dramatic effect whilst offering us a peek at someone more nuanced threatening to break free and shout "Look, I'm not perfect, I don't understand the modern world, but I'm trying... and by the way, I'll still kick your ass with a witty catchphrase whilst I'm doing it."

Even the Warner Bros logo at the start of the film plays its part, appearing in black and white as a segue into grainy footage of front-line action, clips which don't gloss over death, injury and the distress of children and families. Likewise, the use of the jaunty 1961 Don Gibson track 'Sea of Heartbreak' provides a disconcertingly upbeat soundtrack to the imagery, but then the song itself always juxtaposed that cheery sound with its lyrics about lost love. The monochrome visuals slowly change to colour as we are introduced to the character of Highway holding court in a jail cell, telling old war stories before proving he still has what it takes by besting a fellow cellmate. We immediately have a shorthand summary of the character. A war hero who can still pass muster but has found himself so frustrated and perplexed by the modern world and his place in it that he finds himself drinking too much, getting into fights and spending the night behind bars. There are also enough one-liners here to suffice for other whole movies. The stall is well and truly set out.

Whilst the character and dialogue as written by James Carabatsos is somewhat over the top, his script does offer interesting variety in so much as there are three clear sections to the movie: the training of a platoon of

undisciplined marines, the attempted re-romancing of ex-wife Aggie (Marsha Mason, on top form), and the final 20 to 30 minutes of actual battle engagement in Grenada. This could have been confusing, or the romantic sub-plot might have felt like a frustrating intrusion. It might have felt that the ratio of training to genuine front-line conflict might have felt ill-balanced, but none of these are the case. As directed by Eastwood, everything feels as if it belongs and there is a smoothness in the switch from one aspect to another.

Writer Carabatsos was a veteran of the Vietnam War, having been in the 1st Cavalry Division. His script was inspired by the 82nd Airborne Division of American paratroopers who allegedly used a pay telephone and a credit card to call in fire support during the invasion of Grenada. Eastwood was interested in the tale, which featured a Korean War veteran attempting to train a new generation of soldiers in fitness, skills and values. Of course, Eastwood was interested: the principal character would be perfect for him in maintaining his tough guy screen persona whilst also allowing him a level of progression and appropriate aging. It also foreshadowed his later penchant for bringing real life tales of heroism to the screen.

From the outset of the first section of the screenplay, the training, Highway's superior officer Major Powers is set up as an irritant - a pen-pushing officer without combat experience, and one who values image above most things

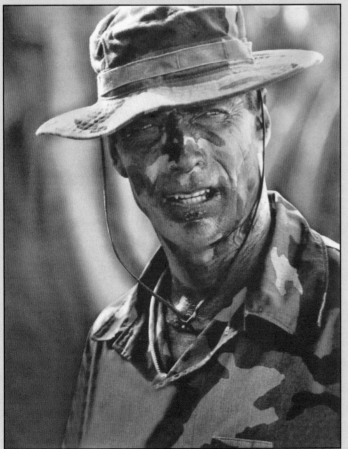

and, worse still, craves victory on the battlefield, something that makes him dangerous. The casting of Everett McGill is perfect. McGill had already proved effective as the monster in reverend's clothing in the Stephen King adaption *Silver Bullet* (1985) and would also stand out as a duplicitous DEA agent in the gritty James Bond film *Licence to Kill* (1989). The role of someone who should be a good guy, but really isn't, was tailor-made for McGill. Major Powers puts Highway in charge of a reconnaissance platoon of ill-disciplined and unmotivated young marines, intending the more experienced soldier to always play second fiddle to the 1st Platoon.

Naturally, Highway works wonders with his men, despite their initial resistance, and there is a lovely moment just before the hour mark when the platoon's reactions show that they are learning and are becoming a tight-knit and efficient team.

In contrast, the romantic sub-plot is sometimes gentler, as Highway attempts to work out where he went wrong with Aggie. This allows for the nice little idiosyncrasy of his character reading women's magazines in the hope of trying to understand the opposite sex. At the same time though, Mason puts in a highly spirited performance as the ex-wife, leading to a fine scene win which she is the one to lose her temper, dropping F-words like grenades before throwing Highway out of her house. This is fun, but also helps Eastwood's development as a conveyor of different characters than usual. Whilst adding drama and pathos, these moments also inject humour into proceedings, something that is ladled on *in extremis* throughout.

The dialogue is fun, though clearly not believable, from the outset. Even in that first sequence in the jail cell, Highway finds time to invite his opponent to "just sit there and bleed awhile, before you feel some real pain." Whilst it can't be denied that Eastwood's most familiar screen persona has made use of witticisms as far back as his 'Dollar' western days of imparting the sensitive reaction of his mule to laughter. Characters such as Dirty Harry Callahan and Josey Wales were never short of a quip before or after violent retribution. Gunny Highway, however, seems to speak more of them than any straightforward expository sentences, and they crop up before, *during*, and after violence action. Even when his is rendered unconscious in battle, the first words on his lips on awakening are part of a recurring series of "this doesn't mean…" *bon mot*.

Thus, the script provides a comfort blanket of Eastwood's Greatest Hits as far as verbal tropes are concerned, and act best as that sense of meta at play that I referred to earlier. They juxtapose the growing self-awareness and age and experience of Eastwood's character.

Perhaps where the comedy sits less effectively is in some of the too pat coincidences that occur, for example, those concerning the character of Stitch (a lively performance from Mario Van Peebles). Stitch is a singing, rapping, guitar-playing wide boy, the figurehead of the malfunctioning bad boys of the platoon. We first meet him following his expulsion from a bar where he was performing on-stage before heckling back the redneck hecklers who don't approve of a black funkster on stage. He boards the same bus as Highway, fair enough, but how likely is it that only spare seat thereon is that which is next to Eastwood's character? And how likely that he would later double-cross Highway, stealing his bus ticket, getting him to pay for his food and drink and then stranding him at a diner in the middle of nowhere. The following morning, Highway is revealed as Stitch's new Gunnery Sergeant/tutor, which is less acceptable in a war drama than it would have been a comedy. Likewise, the appalling appearance, nature and attitude of the men.

And then a sudden thought occurs… this is actually the straight action version of *Police Academy*, or to get more specifically military, how about the 1st and 28th of the bawdy British comedy series of *Carry On…* films! Think about it. A stern stickler for appropriate behaviour is put in command of a slack bunch of ne'er-do-well soldiers, who are not only hopeless by nature, but also deliberately attempt to foil their officer's best intentions. However, he finally earns their respect and vice versa when they learn from him and prove themselves. Yes, that's it - *Heartbreak Ridge* sees Eastwood deliver his version of William Hartnell in *Carry On Sergeant* (1958) or Kenneth Connor in *Carry On England* (1976)!

Luckily, as film critic Roger Ebert pointed out at the time, Eastwood "caresses the material as if he didn't know B movies have gone out of style".

And it's true. Right there in 1986, Clint acted and directed like the old, experienced pro that he was. Acting-wise, he showed a lot without ever seeming to do much of anything: anger, frustration, love, sadness, care. And as a director he brought the best out of the material and offered old, ever true morals and messages. He also

maintained a high level of gung-ho action and attitude, at want point even answering the suggestion that he is too gung-ho by replying "That's what I am!"

Now, I feel that this is probably a predominantly American thing these days (and don't shoot me down, just hear me out). Not everyone in the US is a gun-lover or heavily pro-military, but many are, and I think that is why many American fans will absolutely love the movie. Over here in the UK, we used to make pretty gung-ho films at times - but back when we were either involved in or dealing with the after-effects of the Second World War. I'm not here to say that one way is right or wrong, merely to observe how a slightly different cultural perspective can change how the material is interpreted. In my case, I enjoy it as a very '80s movie with a patriotic nature as old as the hills that can also offer a lot of comedy if looked at from a different angle.

Either way, Eastwood had another hit on his hands, the film taking $121,700,000 in ticket sales and becoming number 18 at the American box office in 1986. Meanwhile, I bought it blind on VHS in the UK, simply because I trusted Eastwood.

His evolutionary step forward into the huge success of his autumn years was a military mission accomplished.

Knightriders

by Rachel Bellwoar

Most people have probably heard of knights in shining armor. George Romero's *Knightriders* (1981) is about knights on shining motorcycles wearing leather armor (because imagine what it would've been like for the stunt riders in this movie if they'd had to wear anything close to a real suit of armor from medieval times).

In a 2013 interview with Romero included on Shout! Factory's Blu-ray release of the film, Romero credits producer Samuel Z. Arkoff with the idea of having the knights ride bikes instead of horses (apparently in Romero's original screenplay, the knights had traditional steeds). It certainly makes for a memorable image when King William (Ed Harris) suddenly switches on the headlight of his bike, subverting expectations that he and his queen Linet (Amy Ingersoll) are mounted on a horse.

Up until that moment, Romero keeps the fact that the film takes place in contemporary times a secret. It certainly doesn't take long for the truth to be revealed, but for a few minutes anyone coming into this movie would be right to assume they're about to watch a period piece, and not necessarily a serious one. The very first scene is of William (or Billy) waking up from a nightmare in the middle of the forest, naked. Linet is lying nude beside him. From there, Billy moves on to self-flagellating himself in a lake, a practice that usually only crops up in movies depicting religious characters, and then (still naked) Billy does some poses with a sword before putting a shirt on.

There's nothing funny about hurting yourself, but there are a lot of images in *Knightriders* that could come across as ridiculous. For the film's detractors, I suppose it never stops being ridiculous and the two and half hour runtime isn't exactly going to endear it to viewers who aren't in love with the characters and would happily watch them do anything, but as someone who falls into the latter camp, what makes it work is how seriously the characters take their profession, and the fact that they are (in the end) professionals.

Knightriders wouldn't be as fun if it was just about a group of people who thought they were King Arthur's court brought back to life in the '80s, but that's not what it's about at all. In fact, all the film's conflicts are born from the fact that this isn't just a hobby for those involved but a business that needs to profit and grow.

That isn't to say Billy's knights are only in it for the money, but because Romero insists on keeping one foot in reality, money is something they have to consider, and that proves especially difficult for Billy to accept. Basically, *Knightriders* is about a traveling Renaissance fair where the main attraction is motorcycle jousting tournaments, but lately Billy's crown has become less secure. For one thing, his rigid moral code is starting to interfere with the group's success (as demonstrated when a crooked cop [Michael P. Moran] tries to hustle them for money and Billy refuses to pay), but there's also the question of whether he's physically up to the task or too stubborn to take time to heal.

It shouldn't have to be said, after all (the fact that they have pre-recorded music instead of trumpet players should be evidence enough), but this isn't medieval times anymore. Billy isn't going to be deposed (or killed) if he

goes on vacation, but that's not how he operates and while, on the one hand, that's part of the troupe's appeal, it could also bring about its downfall.

It would've been easy for the film to simply revel in the excitement of watching motorcycle riders do dangerous tricks and have run-ins with the locals, and there are plenty of sequences involving just that, but *Knightriders* also deals with the "boring" stuff like permits and publicity, and getting to the next gig on time, and that's what makes it compelling. People's livelihoods are at stake, and there are no easy answers.

That's why the rivalry between Billy and Morgan (Tom Savini) is so charged, too. When it comes to names, *Knightriders* isn't always consistent. While some are on the nose (like the running jokes about no one being able to pronounce "Ewain," played by Taso N. Stavrakis), no one is called "Arthur" so it's not immediately clear whether Billy or Alan (Gary Lahti) - Billy's second-in-command - is supposed to be the lead. With a name like Morgan Le Fay, though, there's never any question who Billy's antagonist is, and Morgan quickly presents himself as a threat.

As to whether Morgan's a villain, though, that's not as easy a question to answer. He and Billy certainly disagree on most things and, in terms of casting, it's not a coincidence that Harris is tall and fair while Savini has darker features. The way Morgan is introduced doesn't paint him in the best light either. Basically Morgan wants to try a new weapon in the joust. Alan thinks it's a bad idea but Billy allows it and ends up being the first person Morgan tests it against.

That the weapon ends up being too dangerous comes as no surprise but, in Morgan's defense, he wasn't going to use it without Billy's permission. They're both at fault - Morgan for not showing more restraint, and Billy for letting his ego get the best of him. In all of their arguments, Billy and Morgan both have good points. Morgan is never out-and-out wrong about anything, but while the world of knights is traditionally black and white, *Knightriders* resides in the grey.

To that end, while Billy does come to acknowledge some of his mistakes as leader, it's debatable how much he really learns from them. When the group inevitably splinters, for example, Billy could've been more proactive about convincing his stray knights to return to the fold, but while his choice to rely on faith does work in the end, it's luck - not Billy - which saves the troupe.

One scene that's interesting is the conversation Billy has with one of the troupe's musicians (Donald Rubinstein). While Rubinstein is a significant figure behind the scenes (he's the person who created *Knightriders*' music), his character is never spotlighted before this point, which makes him an odd choice for such an intimate conversation. Just because Rubinstein's musician isn't an established (and therefore important) character to viewers doesn't mean he isn't important to Billy. In fact, it speaks well to the community Billy has fostered that he's able to be vulnerable with a character who (in the context of the movie) is insignificant and not one of his knights.

In the same interview where Romero talks about Arkoff, he also talks about the painting of Harris that was used for the movie poster (Shout! Factory, in turn, used it for the cover of their Blu-ray). Created by fantasy artist Boris Vallejo, it's an objectively good-looking painting. As promotion for *Knightriders*, it completely misses the point. *Knightriders* is first and foremost a film about a community, not one person above the rest, yet you wouldn't know it from the poster.

In fact, one of the best things about *Knightriders* is how integral its female cast members are. On the obvious side, there's Rocky (Cynthia Adler), Billy's only female knight, who could be a token character but whose gender is rarely referenced, and Angie (Christine Forrest), the troupe's primary mechanic. Julie (Patricia Tallman) is Alan's girlfriend and her days dating him are numbered, yet Romero still takes time to flesh out her home life and, for not having too many lines, Ingersoll makes quite the impression as Queen Linet, especially when she has to take charge during Billy's (unexpected) absence. Were this a different movie, this would be the moment when

Morgan would stage a coup. Instead, nobody questions her authority. More importantly, Linet's relationship with Billy is allowed to change without affecting her position in the group. They're not directly linked.

Then there's the epilogue, which is *Knightriders* at its most indulgent, least logical and Billy-centric, so that's not really surprising. Basically Billy crowns Morgan the new king, but it's not an uneasy transition. Billy's behavior afterwards seems unnecessarily extreme. Instead of taking a background role in the troupe, he sends himself into exile. Maybe it's self awareness on Billy's part, that he won't be able to step back and let Morgan reign as he sees fit, but no-one tries to convince him to stay either. From there, it's all about unfinished business for Billy, starting with the deputy who hurt his friend Bagman (Don Berry) and who Billy somehow knows can be found at a fast-food restaurant. Then there's the young boy (Chris Jessel) who Billy initially denied an autograph. Not only is Billy able to walk into his school, bloody and dressed as a knight, without any interference (a prospect that's even more terrifying today), but he proceeds to pass on his weapons to the boy in full view of his class.

Whether or not Billy could've gotten away with either of those encounters in real life, *Knightriders*' excesses are forgivable and fans of Romero's horror films should consider giving *Knightriders* a shot.

MEAN STREETS AND MONSTERS

Q: THE WINGED SERPENT

by James Lecky

A window cleaner is decapitated high on the side of a skyscraper, a sunbather snatched from her rooftop. Something huge, hungry and nasty is preying on the citizens of New York. A man is found flayed in his hotel room, the victim of a ritual killing. Could the deaths be connected? Detectives Shepard and Powell (David Carradine and Richard Roundtree) are assigned to find out.

Meanwhile, petty crook Jimmy Quinn (Michael Moriarty), forced into a botched jewellery heist, flees the bloody scene and, through circumstance, finds himself at the very top of the Chrysler Building where he stumbles across a huge nest and egg. The Aztec god Quetzalcoatl has been reborn in the Big Apple and only Jimmy knows where to find it. . . but he wants a million dollars first.

Q - aka *Q: The Winged Serpent* (1982) - is writer/director Larry Cohen's love letter to New York, a film as firmly fixed in time and place as Woody Allen's *Manhattan* (1979) or Martin Scorsese's *Mean Streets* (1973). Like them, it makes the city practically a character in its own right. In some ways, it's a film of extremes, its gritty urban setting juxtaposed against a wildly fanciful plot, the low-key and realistic central performances contrasted against stop-motion special effects.

Monster pictures developed and flourished in the '50s in the shadow of imminent atomic war and fear of the 'Other'. These creature features eschewed the overtly supernatural, replacing classic movie monsters like Frankenstein, Dracula and the Wolf Man with giant ants (*Them!* 1954), giant spiders (*Tarantula*, 1957) and, of course, the King of the Monsters himself, *Godzilla* (aka *Gojira*, 1954). Humans grew, or indeed shrank, to unnatural size (*The Amazing Colossal Man*, *The Incredible Shrinking Man*, both 1957) and unstoppable alien threats fell from the stars (*The Quatermass Xperiment*, 1955, *Twenty Million Miles to Earth*, 1957 and *The Blob*, 1958). The best of these movies treated their situations, characters and audience with intelligence and sympathy. In the case of *Gojira*, some even managed to inject oblique political commentary along the way.

The genre faltered somewhat in the '60s but would resurface intermittently over the decades (*Valley of the Gwangi*, 1968; *Night of the Lepus*, 1972; *The Food of the Gods*, 1976; *Cloverfield*, 2008, etc).

Q; The Winged Serpent is a monster picture like no other.

Rather than the story showing scientists and military men battling a preternatural threat, it offers for its central character Jimmy Quinn, a former addict turned petty crook and sometime getaway driver who dreams of better things. He's a coward and opportunist who wants to pursue a musical career as a pianist. The 'establishment' figures, best represented by Carradine's Detective Shepard, are quick to give credence to the threat of a huge lizard flying over Manhattan and Shepard himself is convinced there is

more to this admittedly outré situation that meets the eye ("This thing has been prayed into existence.")

Taken out of context, the first act of *Q* could easily be taken for the setup of a gritty crime drama in the way it depicts a small-time crook falling foul of the Mob after a botched robbery. Certainly, Jimmy might have slotted easily into *Mean Streets, Taxi Driver* (1976) or, indeed, *Reservoir Dogs* (1992). But Cohen is making a monster movie, not a slice-of-life, and the pivotal moment of the film is not Jimmy losing the stolen diamonds but his discovery of Quetzalcoatl's nest.

And it is Moriarty's astonishing performance as Jimmy that links the fantastic to the realistic.

Moriarty had come to international prominence with the 1978 miniseries *Holocaust* with his chillingly effective role as Erik Dorf, a fair-weather Nazi who becomes a war criminal. Thereafter, his career would quickly go down the exploitation route. Despite a brilliant performance as Hull Barrett in Clint Eastwood's *Pale Rider* (1985), Moriarty often found himself headlining low-budget horrors, mostly (and to greatest effect) with Cohen. *The Stuff* (1985), *It's Alive III: Island of the Alive* and *A Return to Salem's Lot* (both 1987) mark other examples of Moriarty-Cohen collaborations. He enjoyed something of a career resurgence on *Law and Order* (1990-94), but his reputation for being "difficult" saw him leave the show after four seasons.

Difficult or not (and Cohen has gone on record as saying he never found him so), Moriarty's performance as Jimmy elevates *Q: The Winged Serpent* above many of its '80s equivalents. He often seems to bring out something special in the actors with whom he shares his scenes. Moriarty would also reunite with Cohen in 2006 for the *Masters of Horror* episode *Pick Me Up* playing a coldly efficient serial killer who meets his match.

The scenes between Moriarty and Candy Clark as Jimmy's girlfriend Joan are exemplary, with both actors holding

33

nothing back. Joan loves Jimmy, warts and all, and even gets him an audition as a piano player in the bar where she works (an opportunity which Jimmy utterly fouls up). She is the one person who can see a glimmer of good in him. His scenes with Clark notwithstanding, those with Roundtree and Carradine fizz and crackle with a grounded realism which belies the schlocky foundations of the film.

Much of the kudos has to go to Larry Cohen, an underrated writer and director, who would happily adapt and rewrite scenes to accommodate the talents of his mercurial star. When Jimmy auditions as a piano player in a down-at-heel bar, the inspiration came from Moriarty himself, a real-life talented jazz pianist. He skirts the edge between melody and cacophony, establishing the character in a way that dialogue alone never could (Shepard: "Sounded okay to me." Jimmy: "Yeah? What the fuck do you know?").

Carradine was no stranger to exploitation cinema, either - he'd appeared in the Roger Corman productions *Boxcar Bertha* (1972), *Death Race 2000* (1975) and *Deathsport* (1978), as well as in more prestigious films such as Hal Ashby's *Bound for Glory* (1976) and Walter Hill's *The Long Riders* (1980). He was probably best known for the television series *Kung Fu* (1972-75) and as the eponymous villain in *Kill Bill* (2003). As Shepard, he exudes tough-guy gravitas, whether machine-gunning a giant carnivorous bird or pumping bullets into a deranged cultist in order to save Jimmy's life.

Roundtree, although somewhat underused as Powell, more than matches Carradine in tough-guy terms. As the title character in *Shaft* (1971), he was noted as cinema's first black action hero and continued to play strong characters throughout his career, appearing in *Escape To Athena* (1979), with Roger Moore, Telly Savalas and David Niven and the Cohen-scripted *Maniac Cop* (1988), amongst many others.

Clark, so memorable as Joan, also appeared in *American*

Graffiti (1973) - earning an Oscar nomination in the process - *The Man Who Fell to Earth* (1976), James Foley's tense rural thriller *At Close Range* (1986) and the remake of *The Blob* (1988). She is nothing short of brilliant in her scenes with Moriarty, matching her co-star in every way.

But *Q: The Winged Serpent* belongs to Michael Moriarty. Both he and the film are a lot of fun and both take themselves just seriously enough. Jimmy is a complex character, to say the least, and Moriarty brings out every quirk, every fear, every passion. Yet Quetzalcoatl remains the point of the film. Without the monster (as Cohen himself has said) there is no movie, and by telling his story from the viewpoint of one of its "lowest" characters, Cohen adds to the narrative immeasurably.

In a more traditional monster movie, the focus would have been on Shepard and Powell, their attempts to solve the ritual murders leading to a revelation and then to the death of the monster. And while all these elements exist in *Q*, they are practically in the background, sublimated to the story of Jimmy Quinn.

Writer/producer/director Cohen had been a prolific writer for television - contributing to *The Fugitive*, *The Invaders* and *Columbo* among others - but had cut his cinematic teeth with a trio of blaxploitation films (*Bone*,

1972, *Black Caesar* and *Hell Up in Harlem*, both 1973) before directing a clutch of low-budget horrors including *It's Alive* (1974), *It Lives Again* (1978) and *God Told Me To* (1976). He had been hired to write and direct an adaptation of Micky Spillane's 1947 novel *I, The Jury*, but clashed with the film's producers and was replaced after only a week of shooting. Determined to get back to work as soon as possible, *Q* went into production remarkably quickly. As he explained in Michael Doyle's 'Larry Cohen: The Stuff Of Gods And Monsters': "After the producers of *I, the Jury* fired me, I suddenly decided that I was going to make another picture right away. I thought that if I didn't do something quickly, the stink over my dismissal would hang around… I was no longer employable or something. I already had the script for *Q - The Winged Serpent* sitting idly in my closet." Former army buddy Carradine was drafted in with barely a glance at the script ("I was in a reserve unit and I was shipped down to a small army base in Virginia… David Carradine was also stationed at Fort Eustis, Virginia, at the same time I was, and we became very close friends") and Moriarty was cast via a chance meeting ("I was having lunch with a young actress when I noticed that Michael was sitting at the next table. I'd always admired Moriarty's work, and started telling this actress what a wonderful performer he was. I glanced over and noticed that Moriarty was looking

It's name is Quetzalcoatl… just call it "Q"… that's all you'll have time to say before it tears you apart!

MICHAEL MORIARTY · CANDY CLARK · DAVID CARRADINE · RICHARD ROUNDTREE
AS SHEPARD
IN A LARRY COHEN FILM 'Q'
SAMUEL Z. ARKOFF PRESENTS A LARCO PRODUCTION
MUSIC BY ROBERT O. RAGLAND PRODUCTION EXECUTIVE PETER SABISTON WRITTEN · PRODUCED AND DIRECTED BY LARRY COHEN
SALAH M. HASSANEIN Presentation Released BY UNITED FILM DISTRIBUTION COMPANY   R

over at me. . . He smiled and, a few moments later, I went over to introduce myself. We struck up a conversation and I mentioned that I had a script called *Q* that might contain a good part for him. Moriarty shook my hand and agreed to read it. The very next day he called me, saying he would do the picture and wanted to play the part of Jimmy Quinn.")

The film opens with a series of stunning ariel shots of New York - echoing the San Francisco panorama which graced the opening credits of Don Siegel's *Dirty Harry* (1971) - making that famously turbulent city seem almost tranquil. Indeed, the majority of *Q* takes place far above the streets - from the opening deaths to the bullet-ridden defeat of Quetzalcoatl, in a deliberate nod to *King Kong* (1933), around the summit of the Chrysler Building - with Cohen's camera (courtesy of Fred Murphy and Oliver Wood) capturing architecture that can't be seen from street level.

If the special effects by Randall William Cook and David Allen are a little ragged around the edges, they are nevertheless effective and add a certain loose Harryhausen-esque feel to the proceedings. Although Cohen worked within the confines of small budgets, he always paid for the best he could afford - a truism for most of the low-budget directors in the history of cinema. The monster is revealed in closeups fairly early on - unlike, for example, *Jaws* (1975) - and as such prepares the audience for its first fully fledged appearance flapping across the New York skyline. By this stage, we're prepared to accept what we see and, with retrospect, even appreciate what might have been once mocked. That said, the scene where a sacrificial victim is skinned alive still holds a queasy horror through its use of practical effects.

Q: The Winged Serpent is more concerned with character than premise and Cohen clearly loves the characters (and actors) that inhabit his story. It has been suggested in the past that Cohen was a better writer than director, but at times the cityscape of the film is breathtaking, even slightly terrifying, with its concrete canyons and immense towers, and the film

often manages to belie its low budget ($1.1 million, contrasted with $5 million for the pedestrian *Amityville II: The Possession* or $12 million for John Carpenter's *The Thing*). And, of course, to bang the drum once again, the principal performances are exemplary.

A special mention should be made of Robert Ragland's score which ranges from the eerie title music to the stirring all-out battle with Q. Like the film it accompanies and enhances, Ragland's score shifts tone and mood as necessary - Jimmy's escape from the bungled robbery, for example, is low-key but dramatic, shifting into near gothic when he discovers the nest. The composer provided the soundtrack for a range of low-to-mid budget films in a number of genres including *Mansion of the Doomed* (1976), *Jaguar Lives!* (1979) and a trio of late-period Charles Bronson thrillers - *10 To Midnight* (1983), *Assassination* (1987) and *Messenger of Death* (1988).

Above all, *Q* is a vastly entertaining piece of exploitation cinema.

Sweeping yet personal, ridiculous yet grounded, it is a collision between arthouse and exploitation, taking the best of both and fusing them together into a joyous hybrid.

The legendary William Goldman, that doyen of '70s cinema, wrote in 'Adventures in the Screen Trade' (1983):"Is there no American auteur director? Perhaps there is one. One man who thinks up his own stories and produces his pictures and directs them too… All of this connected with an intensely personal and unique vision of the world. That man is Russ Meyer."

But he might just as validly have mentioned Larry Cohen.

DEATHTRAP

by Martin Dallard

Does Ira Levin's twisty-turny murder-mystery *Deathtrap* enjoy the same success on the big screen as it did on the stage?

Writing a review for a murder mystery can often be a mystery in itself. How does one convey the bare bones of an intricately contrived plot without giving too much away? Well, I'll try to keep the behind-the-curtain goings-on to a bare minimum. I know the film has been around since 1982, but some armchair sleuths may still not have seen this gem of a mystery, so I'll tread as carefully as a cat in a room full of rocking chairs!

Renowned thriller playwright Sidney Bruhl (Michael Caine) has just suffered the worst night of his professional career. His latest comedy thriller *Murder Most Fair*, newly opened at the Music Box Theatre on Broadway, has been mercilessly lambasted by New York's harsh theatre critics. Sidney's only possible recourse is to get blind drunk before returning to his Long Island home early the next morning. He arrives carrying the manuscript of a new play, sent for his perusal by a student who hopes to become a mystery writer. We'll soon discover that the manuscript adds further fuel to the funeral pyre of Sidney's dwindling fame and career.

Sidney's wide Myra (Dyan Cannon) tries to mollify her husband about the previous night's failure. When he tells her all about the manuscript, that it was written by a fledgling student at one of his summer seminars on mystery writing, she tries to spin it in a positive light. She tells him to look upon it as a testimony to his teaching skills. He should feel privileged that the young playwright who wrote it wants to show it to the renowned Sidney Bruhl in the first place. But this doesn't placate the mystery maestro in the slightest.

While listening to his wife, Sidney instead starts to hatch a devious and cunning plan. He half jokes to Myra that he ought to invite the young man over to their house, kill him and then claim the play - titled *Deathtrap* - as his own invention. It becomes apparent Sidney realises the play is a work of genius that not even an untalented theatre director can ruin. If he'd written it himself, he knows his name would be up in lights once again. He'd be rich and talked about, the toast of Broadway, just like in his heyday.

Myra has never heard her husband talk like this before. She realises that the disastrous reception that greeted his play the previous evening must have bruised Sidney's already fragile self-worth worse than she first thought. She jokingly reminds him that world famous Dutch psychic Helga Ten Dorp (Irene Worth) is renting a nearby cottage, readying herself for a book tour and resting up after helping the European police with her amazing powers. If Sidney is harbouring any murderous ideas, they'll almost certainly be picked up by Ms Ten Dorp, so he should cast them out of his mind quick!

Myra suggests that maybe he should think about collaborating with this new playwright, Clifford Anderson (Christopher Reeve). Relenting all too easily, Sidney calls Clifford and invites him over to discuss the play. He tells the new playwright he considers the manuscript a "very promising first draft!"

Clifford, naturally giddy with excitement at the thought of working with his idol, readily agrees. Sidney tells Clifford to bring all relevant paperwork and notes regarding the play, so they have everything to work with. Myra grows a little uneasy - why does her husband want Clifford to bring <u>everything</u> to do with the play? Again Sidney assures her she needn't worry - he tells her he couldn't possibly get away with murder, if that's what she's afraid of. Later that night, Sidney meets his protégé at the railway station and drives him back to meet Myra and possibly to see if they can start a fruitful collaboration.

Will Sidney be able to contain his murderous thoughts, or is he psychotic enough to follow them through to their grisly conclusion? Well, I sure as heck ain't gonna tell ya! Don your deerstalkers and watch the film, and see if you can keep up with the plot which has more twists and turns than the Nurburgring! Who am I to deny you such fun?

Have you ever tried to complete 'The Times' crossword puzzle? Perhaps, like me, you realise after a while the complexity of the puzzle makes you lose interest. Sometimes, the same can be said of murder mysteries. They can be so complex, so overloaded with convoluted red herrings to trip up the viewer, that they become a victim of their own cleverness. Thankfully, that cannot be said of Ira Levin's ingenious play *Deathtrap*. Written and released for the stage in 1978, it was received enthusiastically by theatre audiences and it was only a matter of time before Hollywood came a-calling.

Directed by Sidney Lumet, with a screenplay by Jay Presson Allen, the film version of the celebrated stage play hit the silver screen in March, 1982. It was produced by Burtt Harris, with cinematography by Andrej Bartkowiak and tight editing by Jack Fitzstephens. With the appealing triumvirate of Caine, Cannon and Reeve heading the cast, it looked set to be a sure-fire hit.

Deathtrap was made on a budget of $10 million and went on to make $19 million at the worldwide box office

(about $60 million by today's standards). It was by no means a financial failure but got mixed reviews at the time, which shows that even top-notch talent doesn't necessarily guarantee a surefire hit.

The play and film are labelled as thrillers *about* thrillers, which does indeed get to the nuts and bolts of it all. It does its thing cleverly, never biting the hand that feeds it. It can be said that on a certain level it's a pastiche of what it sets out to imitate - a one-set five-character mystery that leaves us scratching our heads at its cleverness.

A lawyer named Porter Milgrim, played by Henry Jones, is the fifth character in the story. The actor brings his usual air of deferential old-world charm to the role, slightly stuffy but always a reliable voice of reason. He serves as a voice of exposition for the viewer (and, to some extent, to Sidney too), pointing out how certain things and people may not be what they seem on the surface.

The conniving charm of the three leads is what really sells this glorious piece of black comedy hokum. Caine had done a similar film a decade earlier, appearing with Laurence Olivier in *Sleuth*. In *Deathtrap*, he portrays the kind of guy who can't be believed as soon as he opens his mouth. He's narcissistic and self-absorbed, yet Caine's acting prowess makes Sidney somehow… well, likable. You

can't help yourself. In another actor's hands, Bruhl would have come off as irritable and manipulative, yet Caine plays him with aplomb. You hate yourself for liking him.

Cannon won an award for her portrayal of Myra Bruhl, though not the type of award she would have welcomed (a Golden Raspberry for the worst supporting actress performance of 1982). I think the voters missed the point on this one. Cannon's Myra is a wife who wears many metaphorical 'hats' - at once fawning and doting over her husband (she's clearly devoted to him, in spite of the obvious lack of reciprocation) yet also the voice of reason in the relationship. She's the one whose "feet are on the ground and eye is on the cheque book" (as she says at one point). She is overbearing to the point of annoyance, but this seems to come from a need to please her husband. Ultimately, she simply wants to be loved by her man and is deeply troubled by the fact he may have murder on his mind. Wouldn't that make you neurotic too?

Rounding out this unholy trinity is Reeve as Clifford Anderson. He gives a mercurial performance as the playwright wannabe. Reeve learned his craft on the stage before finding meteoric fame as the Man of Steel in *Superman* (1978). There, too, he played a character with more than one face. But here he gets to stretch himself further, entering greyer areas of his character with a portrayal that shows the real scope of his acting bandwidth. Don't take my word for it, see for yourself. I'm sure you'll find Reeve a revelation here. There's a side to Clifford that Reeve never got to explore as Superman. You have to wonder if he was so set in peoples' minds as the Last Son of Krypton that casting him here was detrimental to the success of *Deathtrap*. Perhaps viewers weren't ready to see Reeve in any role that wasn't Superman. For me, this is an insult to an actor who was so much more than the sum of his roles. Hollywood bigwigs at the time very much wanted to shoehorn him into the sort of action-hero roles that were becoming increasingly prevalent in the '80s, but Reeve resisted since he wanted to find parts that would stretch him creatively.

Director Lumet brings the best out of his leads, utilising their range in the confined space of the Bruhl homestead. He'd done a previous film set in a cramped space - *12 Angry Men* (1957), a classic courtroom drama set in a jury room where the twelve men of the title battle it out verbally about the outcome of the man on trial. Likewise *Deathtrap* treats us to long slices of dialogue, showing us the origins on which it is based. There's very little cutting away to other characters, except when Lumet comes in tight on a face in order to ratchet up the tension. Just as the dialogue belies the play the film sprang from, so does the film set which, in its way, could be deemed the sixth member of the cast, virtually a character in and of itself. Confined yet spacious, quirky, with nooks and crannies and old-world weapons and shackles adorning the wall in Sidney's writing room, the Bruhl house is the ultimate 'man cave' for a mystery writer. The home is converted from a windmill, with the creaks and groans from the sails outside adding to the effect. The house breathes with a life of its own. The set design by Tony Walton sells us the notion that the Bruhl home is a *Deathtrap* waiting to happen!

I don't think there's anything I can add without giving the game away. If I've been opaque in my review, trust me, it's with good reason. I want you to find out all the delicious twists and turns for yourself. I hope I've whetted your sleuthing appetite enough to make you want to hunt down this now-classic, cerebral thought-provoker.

As stated earlier, *Deathtrap* gets compared - unfairly in my mind - to Caine's previous foray into the murder mystery genre, *Sleuth*. Both films hark from a critically and financially successful stage play but in all honesty the similarity ends there. *Sleuth* is about a man who gets a kick by playing games on people, often humiliating them. The humiliation leads one victim to seek revenge. *Deathtrap* is more than that, running the gamut of emotions that make us fundamentally human. Chief among these are sloth, avarice, pride and envy. These

emotions can make even the best of us do extraordinarily bad things. And with *Deathtrap*, you'll never have more fun watching those bad things happen!

A WICKEDLY AMUSING WHO'LL DO IT.

IRA LEVIN'S **DEATHTRAP**

MICHAEL CAINE CHRISTOPHER REEVE
DYAN CANNON
in IRA LEVIN'S "DEATHTRAP"
Executive Producer JAY PRESSON ALLEN Associate Producer ALFRED de LIAGRE, JR
Music by JOHNNY MANDEL Produced by BURTT HARRIS
Screenplay by JAY PRESSON ALLEN Based on the stage play by IRA LEVIN
Directed by SIDNEY LUMET

PG PARENTAL GUIDANCE SUGGESTED   From WARNER BROS. A WARNER COMMUNICATIONS COMPANY

sex, lies, and videotape

Voyeurism, Self-Loathing, and What to Do with All the Garbage.

by Sebastian Corbascio

"Do you think I'm pretty? Prettier than Ann?" - Cynthia (Laura San Giacomo) - *sex, lies, and videotape*

sex, lies, and videotape (usually written with all lowercase letters, a rule I'll be using throughout this article) is 34 years old this year. Its director, Steven Soderbergh, is one of the most acclaimed ever and remains indefatigably independent. All the stars of *sex, lies, and videotape* became household names for a time, some still are and deservedly so. The film put Miramax on the map and was the tip of the spear in revolutionizing American independent cinema for the '90s. Taking all that into account, it surprises me that culturally it blips next to zero. It doesn't get talked about nearly enough. This is, after all, the film that predicated everyone filming each other/themselves and then going full frontal public. At least the 2018 Criterion release went some way – though not far enough, I feel - toward lifting it to the standing it deserves. The truth is that *sex, lies, and videotape* happens to be a great film.

The film is like a Russian doll - inside each entity is another entity, and inside the former another, and so on. It's Chekovian in its repression. It's a Kammerspiel with multiple rooms. It has short-story magic to it. It has *dialogue* - no guns, no whizbang special effects, no stars, no product placement, no unjustified back-lighting. It had a $1.6 million budget yet grossed $22 million.

Peter Gallagher was groomed to be a breakout star in a vehicle entitled *The Idolmaker* (1980) but it didn't catch fire. It was almost a decade later, with his spot-on portrayal of smarmy attorney and unfaithful husband John in *sex, lies, and videotape*, that he achieved the bankability the studios had predicted for him years earlier. Gallagher went on to repeat this handsome smarm-boy role in dozens more movies and, in each instance, made it seem brand new. John reveals early in *sex, lies, and videotape* that he has barely strayed from his frat boy roots - he is

first seen spinning his wedding ring like a toy, talking to his friend on the phone about how having a wedding ring is a magnet to women, how he regrets not knowing this during his 'wild years'. He hangs up and rushes out to his lunch-time sexual dalliance. We realize from the start that Gallagher can play a first-rate asshole with dimension in a way that wouldn't fly in the hands of a lesser actor.

sex, lies, and videotape isn't a comedy (although it was inexplicably promoted as one in some markets) but Laura San Giacomo (playing Cynthia, John's adulterous lover and, moreover, the sister of his wife) brings much needed instances of levity. Her Italian ancestry makes a perfect counterpoint to the southern gentility of Andie MacDowell (who plays John's frigid wife, Ann). San Giacomo expertly slips in some southern drawl here and there, but she still feels Noo Yawk overall. In interviews, the actress has stated that the beating heart of the film is the relationship between the sisters - one a 'Madonna', the other a 'Jezebel'. There's a lot of MacDowell's genteel southern upbringing in her performance as Ann. In real life, the topic of sex was considered shameful in her household, something no-one ever discussed. Soderbergh never lays any of this out - there is no exposition, there's not even a road sign, but it's there. After *sex, lies, and videotape*, San Giacomo was briefly the most successful cast member, starring in *Just Shoot Me!* (1997-2003), a sitcom that was perfect for her Anna Magnani-ness. The show ran for 7 seasons in prime time.

James Spader brings his fairest James Dean to *sex lies, and videotape* as John's old college pal Graham, a drifter who makes recordings of women in which they reveal to him their deepest desires and fantasies. He has the face of a sixth-grader which makes it all the more surprising and appealing when he acts. His character comes across like some sort of 'Iago-for-all-seasons'. Graham is trying to overcome the fact that he is a pathological liar and part

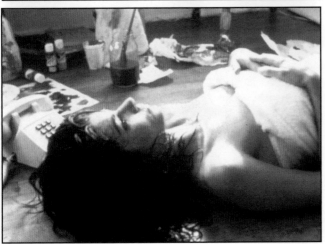

of his 'cure' is to tell the truth at all times. His line delivery is cautious, like he's walking on proverbial eggshells. When telling the truth, he sounds like he's delivering bad news.

MacDowell's only previous feature role had been as Jane in *Greystoke: The Legend of Tarzan, Lord of the Apes* (1984) where her lines were looped by Glenn Close. She was a high fashion model working for Calvin Klein and L'Oréal. The clang around the water cooler was that she couldn't act and Soderbergh was almost violently opposed to even considering her. He wanted Elizabeth McGovern to play Ann, but MacDowell's audition brought the house down (Soderergh later waxed poetically that one of her superpowers was that she could blush on cue).

sex, lies, and videotape gave the fledgling Miramax unlimited street cred. It was the beginning of the beginning for founding producers Harvey and Bob Weinstein. The sterling contributions of Soderbergh, MacDowell, San Giacomo, Gallagher, Spader and cinematographer Walt Lloyd helped Miramax become a trademark for movies with a certain touch for the decades that followed. The big studios of yore had always had their specialties (MGM for musicals, Warner Bros. for crime dramas, etc.) and Miramax became known for good scripts and peak performances in independent cinema. Bob and Harvey had a great eye and nose for what would get sophisticated asses on seats.

The opening credits of *sex, lies, and videotape* are shaky white on black, as if they are an animation experiment. There are two opening title cards, both given two seconds of screen time, followed by the opening shots which are not accompanied by any credits. We can tell instantly that this is an independent movie, done on a budget that could maybe pay for landscaping a backyard (well, a Beverly Hills backyard at any rate).

The first shot is a close-up of gravel whizzing by, shot at full speed from a camera positioned dangerously close to the ground. We hear guitar music by the great Cliff Martinez, doing an ominous minor-key *Rocky Mountain Breakdown* solo guitar (unlike most films, we never hear the opening theme again), which stops right when the gravel stops whizzing by. We learn the driver is Graham (Spader), travelling to Baton Rouge, Louisiana, in a big car from yesteryear. He stops at a gas station - a noir trope straight out of *The Postman Always Rings Twice* - and takes a sponge bath in the bathroom before going to visit his old pal John and John's wife Ann. They can't deny Graham their hospitality, but it's been nine years since the guys' crazy college days and a *lot* has changed. When Graham and Ann first clasp eyes on each other, it's not sexually charged like we might expect from our knowledge of noir movies past. But Graham's gears are spinning fast, and we've already seen that in the trunk of his car (another noir trope - gangsters pack their wares, and the occasional victim, in their trunks) he carries a video camera. We wonder what purpose the video camera will serve in the story (certainly, the marketing at the time mis-sold us into expecting some high-class porn... there is, in fact, no nudity in the entire film and when Soderbergh screened the rushes and first cut, one producer famously cried out: "Where are the tits!?")

Ann does her best to act the typical southern housewife, sittin' and talkin' a spell, before Graham abruptly starts asking personal questions like "How do you like being married?" A few questions in, Ann finds herself feeling strangely comfortable with this Velvet Underground fan. She gets a whiff of danger from Graham, but also senses a portal to something that will at least take her out of her present state of suspended animation. A lesser actor might have come across as creepy, but in Spader's hands Graham is extremely engaging. We can't figure out why, and therein lies the magic. That's true of the whole film - in the hands of a less capable cast, the whole thing might have fallen flat.

Strangely, there is no reunion scene between Graham and John. Soderbergh's first scene of the two old college buddies is at the dinner table, where John puts on the middle-class horse-and-pony act and seems somewhat displeased that Graham hasn't joined the fun of the adult world. Clearly, John and Graham's relationship is no longer the same, nor is it the center of the action. The presence of Ann, continuously counter-jabbing John's little asides, shows that she is clearly not a pushover. The set-up is expertly done. It's a slow burn. At one point, Ann complains to her therapist about what to do about all the garbage that's piling up - a most unsubtle metaphor for

the way her life is going in general.

Soderbergh heightens the tempestuous undercurrent of these lives with highly effective but sparingly used shots. When we see Cynthia having an orgasm, Soderbergh uses a reverse zoom - perhaps the most famous and overused whizbang in-camera effect since its inception in *Vertigo* (and its regurgitation in about 97% of all student films). Here it feels new. Cynthia has her orgasm sitting up - it isn't John giving it to her, rather a post coital orgasm with John crashed-out beside her. The camera tilts with Cynthia as she lays back down, except when she is laid down, we see her in vertical profile. She takes a deep breath and says: "You can go now." John chuckles and gets up and, we're assuming, gets dressed. It's an afternoon tryst a la *Psycho*, but, in this case, completely loveless with no future and no remorse. Why are they doing it? Who knows? Probably to inject some excitement into their faux '50s existence. The overall impression is that Cynthia is turned-on by the situation while John is merely her fluffer.

Soderbergh's filming of the video playback scenes, with the lines and flicker, add a gothic texture. The use of sound is extraordinary. Often, it leads to pivotal scenes or is used to jar us, contrasting bravely with Ann's spic-and-span home, life and libido. Sound editor Larry Blake worked with Soderbergh on many subsequent projects and it's easy to see why.

The other real success of the film is Soderbergh's editing. *sex, lies, and videotape* is a perfect blend of talking movie magic and silent movie magic. The camera has a huge crush on MacDowell - she had already moved millions as a model and her visage is beautifully exploited in this film. In the scenes where she goes to look at Graham sleeping on the couch, photographer Lloyd (who later shot *Short Cuts*) doesn't go overboard with the chiaroscuro and lets MacDowell do her job. The close-up of her looking at Graham is the best in the film - we see that she's attracted to him, but we see too that she fears that attraction and has no idea how to make sense of her feelings. She lingers, then retreats. Graham's eye opens... and cut. The scene is underpinned by minor-key ambient music. All the elements do their bit.

Another edit that works fabulously is when Ann goes to Graham's house to confront him. She gets in her car, and, without starting the car, covers her ears. The sound of a compactor or large machinery wells up as she closes her eyes. There's a jump cut to her where she is parked, ears covered, eyes closed, compactor noise gone. Soderbergh does not provide an establishing shot, but rather stays on her in the car. She gets out and we suddenly realize she is in front of Graham's home. She is as surprised as we are. This is a confident and highly original piece of trickery from the 26-year-old director-writer-editor (this sequence seems to have no precedent... I wonder if it might be wholly original).

What follows, the finale, is devastating. To describe it here would not do it justice - suffice to say all of the elements (sound, cutting, acting, lighting) come together amazingly. It's an amalgamation and a promise fulfilled. Gallagher would later enjoy describing the historic 1989 Sundance screening, where the young and nerdy Soderbergh came out to introduce the film and invited distributors to talk to him afterwards if they were interested in picking up the film - as the end credits rolled, the entire audience sat gobsmacked at what they had just seen.

The coda harkens back to the ending of *The Graduate* in the sense that the protagonists get everything they desire, but now what? What obstacles and terrors does the future hold for the star-crossed lovers? Graham is still somewhat of a fop. Ann must acclimatize to a lower standard of living. Orgasm is the arbiter, the decider to all the big stuff. What next?

Just about everyone involved in *sex, lies, and videotape* went on to immediate stellar careers, except Soderbergh himself. MacDowell starred in many important films right after including *Short Cuts* and uber-favorites *Groundhog Day* and *Four Weddings*

and a Funeral. San Giacomo went on to *Pretty Woman* and *Just Shoot Me!* and was almost in *The Godfather III*, only to be replaced at the last minute by Sofia Coppola. Spader's career needs no recap; nor does Gallagher's. Walt Lloyd lensed *Short Cuts*. Composer Martinez worked with Soderbergh closely for years. But Soderbergh had a little longer to wait - his career right after *sex, lies, and videotape* didn't shoot into space like it deserved. He made a few decent projects, but his stars didn't truly align until two of his pictures - *Erin Brockovich* and *Traffic* - were nominated for Best Picture Academy Awards in the same year (2000).

sex, lies, and videotape got the vaunted Criterion treatment in 2018, as have a number of other Soderbergh films, but the release garnered very little hullabaloo. For such a historic, ground-breaking, career-making film, it doesn't get heralded the way it should. This is borderline shameful. *sex, lies, and videotapes*' gravitas, its performances, its analog technical wizardry, have not faded even a little since it was released. It's an '80s classic that should be showered with praise at every opportunity.

Caddyshack

by Ernie Magnotta

There are certain films that you watch and enjoy but then don't revisit until years later. Then there are those you never tire of, ones you find yourself constantly quoting dialogue from. Every time you come across them playing on TV, you stop what you're doing and watch them through to the end. The 1980 Harold Ramis comedic masterpiece *Caddyshack* definitely falls into the latter category.

Young Danny Noonan (Michael O'Keefe) has a problem. His father wants him to go to college, otherwise he'll pull some strings and get Danny a job at the local lumberyard. This is the last thing Danny wants. The trouble is Danny has no money for college and, although he longs for a better life, has no idea what he wants to do. Right now, he's happy enough just drifting along, working part-time as a golf caddy at the elitist Bushwood Country Club and hanging out with his girlfriend Maggie (Sarah Holcomb) and his friend/rival D'Annunzio (Scott Colomby). While at Bushwood, he comes into contact with friendly, laid-back millionaire Ty Webb (Chevy Chase), snobbish Judge Smails (Ted Knight), and slobbish but loveable tycoon Al Czervik (Rodney Dangerfield) whose crude antics drive the uptight Smails crazy. Meanwhile, the dimwitted greenskeeper Carl Spackler (Bill Murray) is on a do-or-die mission to kill a

gopher that's destroying Bushwood's golf course.

After reluctantly sucking up to Smails in order to possibly get a caddy scholarship, Danny is asked by Ty and Al to help them win a $160,000 bet by replacing the injured Al in a golf tournament against the condescending judge and his right-hand man Dr. Beeper (Dan Resin). Will Danny play it safe and go for the scholarship or will he gamble his entire future by humiliating Smails and hopefully winning the tournament and the money?

Directed by Second City improvisational comedy troupe alumnus Harold Ramis and written by Brian Doyle-Murray (Bill's older brother), Douglas Kenney (co-founder of the legendary and groundbreaking National Lampoon magazine) and Ramis, *Caddyshack* is a hilarious comedy which pits the snobs against the slobs. It also happens to contain some of the most quotable lines in film history including the immortal: "Be the ball."

The screenplay was based on Ramis' and Doyle-Murray's memories of working as caddies when they were teenagers. Originally the film was going to focus on the young caddies, with the characters of Danny and D'Annunzio taking center stage. But when the uproarious improvisational skills of Chase, Dangerfield and Murray became evident,

the heavyweight comedians' characters were enlarged and became the main focus of the movie. Scenes involving Danny were cut down considerably and, unfortunately, D'Annunzio was almost eliminated from the story altogether. The character of Maggie was also greatly reduced in order to shoot and add scenes featuring the gopher. Originally "Mr. Gopher" was going to remain off screen, but a mechanical puppet created by special effects master John Dykstra ended up featuring in numerous scenes.

Ramis shot *Caddyshack* in various Florida locations throughout the autumn of 1979. Besides filming the hysterical pool sequence where he successfully recreates the swimmers-fleeing-the-water scene from *Jaws* as well as shooting an insane and now classic action sequence of Al Czervik running amok with his yacht, Ramis also crafted many character-building scenes such as Danny riding his bike to work while admiring and longing for the affluent houses he passes. The first-time director is also responsible for having the talent and intelligence to allow his amazing stable of comedians to freely improvise their scenes whenever they feel it necessary.

For instance, when it comes to the character of Carl, the awesome Bill Murray (later an Oscar nominee for *Lost in Translation*) not only improvised every scene he was in, but in doing so he created an iconic and riotous character. The scenes between him and Mr. Gopher are like something out of a Wile E. Coyote/Road Runner Looney Tunes cartoon.

The great Chevy Chase shines as Zen playboy Ty Webb, playing the character with a hilarious aloofness. (The famous massage oil scene between Ty and Judge Smails' gorgeous niece was also completely improvised by the actors.) Since 1980, Chevy has consistently gone on record in saying that Harold Ramis gave him the attitude to play Ty Webb.

The marvelous Rodney Dangerfield seemed born to play loveable, blue collar turned *nouveau riche* Al Czervik. There isn't one scene where the powerhouse comedian doesn't deliver. Ironically, on the first day of shooting, Rodney was upset because no-one was laughing. Rodney thought he was terrible and told this to co-star Scott Colomby who assured Rodney that he was great. Colomby also told him that the reason no-one was laughing was because if they did it would ruin the sound take. Contrary to his famous catchphrase "I don't get no respect", the brilliant Rodney had the respect of everyone involved in the film.

The late, great Ted Knight gives an unbelievably spot-on performance as the pompous Judge Smails. Knight expertly plays the character in such a way that he has the audience laughing at his numerous negative qualities thereby making Smails a character we love to hate while, at the same time, holding his own against comedic geniuses Murray, Chase and Dangerfield.

The incredible acting talent doesn't stop there. *Caddyshack*'s original lead characters of Danny, D'Annunzio and Maggie, although cut down, are still memorably portrayed by O'Keefe, Colomby and Holcomb respectively. O'Keefe makes Danny a regular kid who the young audience can fully relate to. He comes off as humorous, likeable and, most of all, real. Colomby plays working class, Italian-American D'Annunzio as somewhere between friend and semi-harmless enemy. I've known a few guys like D'Annunzio in real life, and Colomby totally nails it. Holcomb also shines as girl-next-door Maggie. Although her role was severely cut down, we get to see her acting chops in the scene where she fears she may be pregnant.

The sidesplitting movie is also loaded with a ton of excellent supporting actors/familiar faces such as the

lovely Cindy Morgan as the insatiable Lacy Underall, the always welcome Brian Doyle-Murray as the no-nonsense but likeable Lou, and John F. Barmon who is unforgettable as Judge Smails' spoiled and disgusting grandson Spaulding.

Caddyshack also features Dean Resin as the goofy Dr. Beeper, Henry Wilcoxon as soon-to-be atheist Bishop Pickering and, as Mrs. Smails, Lois Kibbee. They all add immensely to the madness.

Last, but not least, jazz musician extraordinaire Jackie Davis makes a brief appearance as the hard-working but put-upon Bushwood employee Smoke Porterhouse, and highly recognizable character actor Albert Salmi can be spotted as Danny's father.

Close to the end of shooting, producer Jon Peters realized that two of the film's biggest stars, Bill Murray and Chevy Chase, who both rose to fame on NBC TV's immortal sketch comedy/variety show *Saturday Night Live*, did not have a single scene together. To rectify this, Ramis, Kenney, Murray and Chase quickly wrote one (which has nothing to do with the film's plot) during a lunch break. They shot it later that day!

Peters also suggested building a mechanical gopher in order to save time and money. He anticipated it would be considerably less problematic than using a live, trained one.

The catchy and now classic Kenny Loggins theme song

I'm Alright perfectly complements many of the onscreen characters (especially Danny). The film also features music from other well-known but diverse artists, such as Journey, Earth Wind & Fire, Tchaikovsky and John Williams (whose iconic *Jaws* theme is used in the aforementioned and highly memorable 'Baby Ruth' pool scene) as well as a wonderful score by Grammy-winning composer Johnny Mandel.

Caddyshack inevitably produced a sequel (1988's *Caddyshack II*), but the less said about that the better. Ramis was against the sequel all along and, after being talked into co-writing the first draft of the screenplay, he unsuccessfully tried to get his name taken off the movie.

Caddyshack is a riotous joy. It gets better with each viewing and will have you roaring with laughter every time you see it. Released by Warner Bros. on July 25th, 1980, this $6 million budgeted movie grossed almost $40 million at the box office.

Some reviews have said that the film wanders from having too many storylines, and also that it is too loosely written in its determination to allow lots of improvisation. However, I must disagree with this. I believe these are the very reasons the movie is a beloved comedy classic. In fact, the improvisation, the looseness and the multiple character arcs and story threads are the very reason why *Caddyshack* is, and will forever be, considered a cinematic hole-in-one.

(This article is lovingly dedicated to the memories of Harold Ramis, Rodney Dangerfield, Ted Knight, Douglas Kenney, Dean Resin, Henry Wilcoxon, Jackie Davis and Albert Salmi. R.I.P.)

48

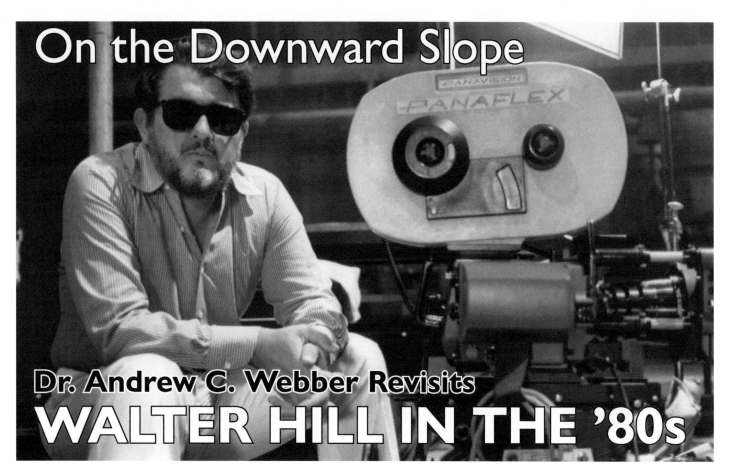

On the Downward Slope

Dr. Andrew C. Webber Revisits
WALTER HILL IN THE '80s

It's slightly surprising that the prolific and talented American director Walter Hill was not considered a movie brat. He had all the trappings: white, male, bearded, born in California in 1942. Perhaps he was just that little bit too old to fit in? And maybe just a little too traditional? Plus, he loved westerns.

Hill made films very much in the classical style and his favourite genre was one the movie brats steered very clear of - Peter Fonda's excellent *Easy Rider* follow-up *The Hired Hand* (1971) was one of the few oaters made by directors who ushered in the New Hollywood of the '70s. Spielberg, Milius, De Palma, Malick, Scorsese, Bogdanovich, Schrader and Lucas (to name a few of the hot new directors who came to be known as the Movie Brats) never made a cowboy flick and, whilst I have previously argued that the '70s was actually a great decade for the genre, most of the decade's key westerns were actually being made by old hands like Robert Aldrich, Michael Winner, Arthur Penn, Howard Hawks, Blake Edwards, Don Siegel, Burt Kennedy, Sam Peckinpah and Richard Fleischer. Yes, you could argue that *Star Wars* is a western set in space, but it also has a Death Star and aliens (not exactly common western tropes) and while John Carpenter's *Assault on Precinct 13* heavily borrows the genre's codes and conventions, it's also got gangs, cops and is set in LA (with added *Rio Bravo* touches thrown in for good measure).

Hill came to prominence as the writer of Sam Peckinpah's *The Getaway* and Robert Culp's little-seen and rather underrated *Hickey and Boggs* (both 1972), John Huston's *The Mackintosh Man* (1973) and the belated *Harper* sequel *The Drowning Pool* (1975), the latter two both starring Paul Newman.

His debut as director was the Depression-set drama *Hard Times* (aka *The Street Fighter*) in 1975, starring Charles Bronson and James Coburn (two very old skool '70s stars) which he followed with the brilliant Ryan O'Neal neo-noir *The Driver* (1978) featuring a never-better Bruce Dern, the impossibly gorgeous (and apparently age-defying) Isabelle Adjani, plus some of the greatest car chases of the '70s (which is saying something of a decade that also gave us *Two-Lane Blacktop*, *Vanishing Point*, *The French Connection*, *The Seven Ups*, *Dirty Mary, Crazy Larry* and *Freebie and the Bean*). As producer, Hill hit paydirt with Ridley Scott's *Alien* (1979), and in the same year his third movie as director, the controversial gang drama *The Warriors*, was also released. In the UK, *The Warriors* was originally screened accompanied by a truly dreadful Leonard Rossiter-starring comedy-short entitled *Le Petomane* - the story of a real-life French cabaret artist whose performances revolved around acts of self-induced flatulence, which is probably the real reason why seats were slashed and cinemas trashed across the country (if, indeed they ever were).

In the '80s, after a supremely good start, his career followed a generally downhill trajectory. His journeyman style translated itself into ever more flaccid material from 1985 onwards. However, at the beginning of the decade,

Hill was a man on fire. Regularly aided and abetted by a team of trusted collaborators - notably musician Ry Cooder, writer David Giler and producer Larry Gross - Hill made a trio of great movies that few '80s directors bettered (although Tony Scott would give him a run for his money in the '90s).

The Long Riders (1980) is an excellent, lean western which was sold on the basis of its stunt casting and bank-rolled by United Artists, who foolishly thought that Michael Cimino's *Heaven's Gate* (which they were also funding at enormous cost) was going to bring about a western revival (we all know what happened there). *The Long Riders* retells the oft-told tale of the James Gang and their riotous ride from ragged glory to untimely death. Interestingly, theirs is very much a family tale with brothers and twins playing a significant part in it. Therefore Hill decided to cast real life brothers in key roles: the Keach brothers, Stacy and James (who co-wrote and co-produced the movie) play gang leaders Frank and Jesse; the Carradine brothers, David (impeccably cool), Keith and the less recognisable Robert are the Youngers; Dennis and Randy Quaid are the Millers, and the film's villains Charley and Robert Ford are played by *Spinal Tap's* Christopher Guest and his brother Nicholas. The story had previously been told by Philip Kaufman in the under-rated *The Great Northfield Minnesota Raid* (1972) in which Cole Younger was played by Cliff Robertson and Jesse James by Robert Duvall. That film went relatively overlooked at the time of its release.

In some ways, it is similar to Blake Edwards' *Wild Rovers* (1971), which was criticised at the time for its obvious nods to superior westerns made by the likes of John Ford and Sam Peckinpah. In *The Long Riders*, we have a lot of slow motion action and a fair bit of graphic violence which naturally echoes *The Wild Bunch* and, similarly, the family idea evokes Ford. The costume design (it's there in the title) pays tribute to the magnificent dust jackets Leone made fashionable in *Once Upon a Time in the West* (1968). I remember absolutely loving this film when I saw it on its first release and re-watched, over 40 years later, it still impresses. It looks great (the cinematography is by Hill regular Ric Waite, who would later also shoot Milius' *Red Dawn* in 1984). The acting is pretty strong (it's pity that we see so little of James Keach hereafter - his only

subsequent appearance of note is as a prison warder in James Mangold's Johnny Cash biopic *Walk in the Line* in 2005) and there's a muddy neo-western lived-in quality to it, which makes it feel like it belongs in the mid '70s rather than the early '80s. In addition, Ry Cooder's traditional music (this was his first ever soundtrack) works really well, adding to the authentic atmosphere and, whilst this may well be *yet another* western about masculinity and fraternal loyalty, Pamela Reed in her debut as prostitute Belle Starr also makes an impression and is eminently watchable in her few scenes.

The movie was swiftly followed by Hill's taut Vietnam parable *Southern Comfort* (1981), which reunited him with Keith Carradine and a superb ensemble cast including granite-jawed Powers Booth, Peter Coyote, Fred Ward and Brion James (best known as the replicant Leon in *Blade Runner*). The premise is a group of Louisiana guardsmen are on a training expedition in the deep South swamplands (armed only with blanks) and, in true *Deliverance* style, realise that the locals are far from friendly after they steal a few canoes to traverse a river that has appeared out of nowhere on their outdated maps. This is a really strong men-on-a-mission movie which gives Carradine a rare chance to take a central role and its investigation of masculinity in crisis is expertly handled, as you'd expect from a director well-versed in this particular topic.

Not since "Deliverance"...

It's the land of hospitality...unless you don't belong there.

SOUTHERN COMFORT

Southern Comfort by Aaron Stielstra

Cooder's stunning soundtrack is, once again, an integral part of the overall effect (it ensures that the film hasn't dated, unlike some of Hill's later works which rely on the synthesisers that became popular during the period) and there are many great scenes, including the extended *Apocalypse Now* style conclusion intercutting a dramatic confrontation between the surviving guardsmen and their pursuers with the ritualistic slaying of an animal and a Cajun community at play.

Andrew Lazlo's cinematography captures the strangeness and beauty of the swamplands (he'd shot Hill's *The Warriors* and would follow it with, amongst others, Richard T. Heffron's Mike Hammer thriller *I, the Jury* and Ted Kotcheff's *First Blood*) and the fraying relationships between the men in the platoon are engrossing and supremely well acted. *Southern Comfort* is undeniably a great film from the early '80s and may well be Hill's masterpiece.

Like *The Long Riders*, the brilliance of San Francisco-set smash hit *48 Hrs.* which Hill then directed (with a fair bit of studio interference) in 1982 is also down to its casting. This one, of course, made a huge star of Eddie Murphy (and didn't hurt Nick Nolte's career either - he plays the hard drinkin' and heavy smokin' maverick cop Jack Cates). Yes, it's yet another mismatched buddy cop movie but arguably it is THE mis-matched buddy cop movie. *Warriors* James

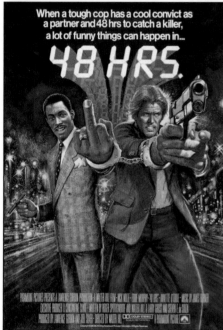

When a tough cop has a cool convict as a partner and 48 hrs to catch a killer, a lot of funny things can happen in...

48 HRS.

Remar (who'd appeared briefly in *The Long Riders* as a Native American) and the crazy David Patrick Kelly are back as the decidedly nasty villains; the profane interplay between the two stars is very funny and the 21-year-old Murphy, as hustler Reggie Hammond, burns up the screen. It may be remembered as a *Beverly Hills Cop* style romp but, in fact, it's a tightly directed, violent thriller with a few humorous asides. The Murphy shtick might not work for sensitive modern audiences but this one definitely kicks opens the door for risk-taking black American comedy, which Pryor had nudged ajar in his *Richard Pryor Live in Concert* film of 1977. Obvious highlights include the memorable (largely improvised)

scene in Torchy's redneck bar in which the white trash drinkers are given a taste of their worst nightmare by an Armani suited and booted Murphy; a bravura single-take sequence early on in a police station (featuring a blink and you'll miss him cameo from *Southern Comfort's* Brion James); James Horner's slightly heavy-handed sax-heavy soundtrack (he'd just worked on *Star Trek: The Wrath of Khan*); a great chase in the Church Street subway station and a hummable, catchy theme tune *The Boys are Back in Town*, written by Brian O'Neal and performed by The Busboys (who also appear in the movie). The original choices for the main roles - Clint Eastwood and Richard Pryor - would, no doubt, have given the material an interesting spin but it's hard to see how they could have bettered the gruff, bear-like Nolte and the too-cool-for-school Murphy. *48 Hrs.* is indecently entertaining and one of the '80s most purely enjoyable movies.

It's interesting to also note that all three of his early '80s films were awarded X certificates in the UK - Hill was never one to back away

from violence and harsh language (although he rarely included sex). His movies are grown-up entertainment - the kind we see so few of all these years later.

Streets of Fire is Hill's 1984 rock 'n' roll fable (it was originally intended as the first part of a trilogy), an overblown, big budget semi-musical starring 18 year old Diane Lane (she of Coppola's *The Outsiders* and *Rumble Fish,* both 1983) as a convincing (even though she mimes the numbers) rock singer Ellen Aim, who is kidnapped at the beginning of the movie by evil motorcycle gang The Bombers (who could have easily been in *The Warriors*). Her saviour, rifle-wielding tough guy Tom Cody, is played by Michael Paré who, to be honest, can't quite cut the mustard - even though he tries. Paré's career never took off, although he was later brilliantly cast by Sofia Coppola in a small but significant role in her excellent 1999 debut *The Virgin Suicides*. Hill had previously shown himself to be adept when it came to musical sequences in his films (the Cajuns at the end of *Southern Comfort* and The Busboys "live" in *48 Hrs.*) so, with the benefit of hindsight, his decision to want to make a musical fantasy is not as unexpected as it perhaps appeared back in 1984. *Streets of Fire* moves along at a fair old pace. It's also a chance for Hill to centralise his female characters (who had usually been given short shrift in his work. *48 Hrs.* especially is unlikely to be heralded by feminists). In addition to Lane, there's a small comic role for Amy Madigan, who'd go on to make a major impact in *Field of Dreams* in 1989. Here she plays Paré's (lesbian?) hard-as-nails sidekick McCoy (*"I told ya, you're not my type,"* she says, twice, just in case he and we might have missed it). Token-female *Warrior* Deborah Van Valkenburgh plays Reva, Cody's diner-owning sister (unfortunately a *very* under-written role). At the end of the day, Lane is little more than a Proppian princess, threatened by marauding males and needing to be rescued by her prince, but she struts her way through the musical numbers with aplomb (especially *Bat out of Hell's* Jim Steinman's infuriatingly hook-line heavy *Nowhere Fast*) and possesses a sassy sexuality throughout. Although Hill's go-to guy Ry Cooder is back on soundtrack duty, most of the songs (which he didn't write and which were overseen by Jimmy Iovine) are a little grating, capitalising as they do on the big-hair excessive guitar rock which was so unaccountably popular in America at the time. You yearn for some pure rock 'n' roll, rather than the airbrushed 'rawk' which the film is built around, but it's good to see cult band The Blasters as themselves, playing in (yet another) club called Torchies and fictional group The Sorrels perform a great acappella Do Wop number midway through.

A youthful Willem Dafoe turns up (in fetish gear) as the baddie Raven, his eccentric performance echoing the work he did on Bigelow's *The Loveless* (1982) and later in Friedkin's

To Live and Die in LA (1985). You also get the chance to see *Ghostbusters'* unlikeable Rick Moranis as Billy Fish, Lane's cynical manager (and improbable love-interest) and likeable cult actor Bill Paxton as a barman with an improbably huge DA (the '50s inspired 'look' of the movie is one of its pleasures).

In fact, the production design (by John Vallone, who'd worked on all of Hill's '80s films except *The Long Riders*) is spectacular - the lavish studio sets, which made the movie so expensive to make, remind you of *Blade Runner* with a hint of Coppola's *One from the Heart* (another '80s musical which died a death in spite, or perhaps because, of a superb score by Tom Waits. It's a bit of a shambles but there's ambition here and a snazzy visual stylishness that you might not have expected from Hill: the film was shot by Andrew Laszlo, who'd worked with him on *The Warriors* and *Southern Comfort* and had just shot Kotcheff's *First Blood* in 1982. *Streets of Fire* is edited, in full-on MTV style, by James Coblentz, Freeman A.

Tonight is what it means to be young.

STREETS OF FIRE

A Rock & Roll Fable.

Davies and Michael Ripps. It was a financial flop, however, costing over $14 million but barely scraping back $8 million at the box office.

Streets of Fire does feature a few typical Hill touches, even if the violence is toned down: scenes in busses and on subway trains, with motorcycles standing in as horses but, at the same time, seems to herald in a new era of slickness (a sort of *cinema du look* US-style) which, arguably, blights a lot of movies made in the decade (it certainly dates them).

Paré completists might like to know that in 2008 Albert Pyun (the king of straight-to-video soft-core trash) made *Road to Hell,* an unofficial sequel, which reunited Paré and Van Valkenburgh. Watch it if you dare.

The Richard Pryor New York-set family-friendly comedy remake *Brewster's Millions,* which he made next in 1985 (the seventh version of the story), could have been directed by almost anyone but it passes the time in a sub-*Trading Places* kind of way - presumably Hill needed to play it safe after the financial mess of *Streets of Fire?* Pryor's genius was rarely well served by Hollywood (*Blue Collar* the notable exception), in spite of the fact that his stand-up routines were amongst the greatest comedy moments ever captured on screen. Here, he plays a naive

Hackensack Bulls baseball player charged with spending a $30-million inheritance in thirty days. *Brewster's Millions* also features John Candy as Pryor's pal Spike Nolan, hot off Ron Howard's big hit *Splash!* He would later find fame in *Planes, Trains and Automobiles* (alongside Steve Martin) for director John Hughes in 1987. Candy died of a drug, booze and binge-eating heart attack in 1994, aged 43. Coke-freak Pryor outlived him, but finally, after years of suffering from MS ("*More shit,*" he quipped) also succumbed to a heart attack in 2005 at the age of 65.

Along for the ride are tough guy actor Jerry Orbach as the Bulls' coach (he'd just been in Lumet's brilliant *Prince of the City* and would later appear in, amongst others, *Dirty Dancing, Someone to Watch Over Me* and *Crimes and Misdemeanors*), Pat Hingle, veteran Hume Cronyn and, in a tiny role as a sports commentator, former footballer and future born-again Christian (and Mayor of Fresno) Alan Autry who, as Carlos Brown, had played the traumatised guardsman 'Coach' Bowden in *Southern Comfort.* Interestingly, he'd changed his name after tracking down and reuniting with his estranged father on *that* film's shoot, a man who'd abandoned his family when the actor was an infant but, presumably, the reunion worked out, prompting him to readopt his birth name thereafter.

Hill apparently regretted making this one (it has none of the western qualities he'd previously brought to the mix and you have to wonder what drew him to the project apart from the pay cheque) and a lost comedy classic it most certainly is not. Yes, Hill *was* able to handle funny

moments in his films, but he was certainly not a director noted for his sense of humour. *Brewster's Millions* confirms this, in spite of having yet another scene set in a downtown bar called, you guessed, Torchy's.

1986's *Crossroads*, inspired by the legend of how blues guitarist Robert Johnson sold his soul to the devil and featuring *Outsider* and *Karate Kid* Ralph Macchio alongside the likeable Joe Seneca, was a Ry Cooder pet project but went virtually unreleased in the UK (it's the only one of Hill's films I had to watch for the first time for this article). It feels a bit out of place for a Hill film, with its supernatural elements and relatively gentle atmosphere. Unfortunately it

becomes increasingly risible as it goes on. 'People' magazine commented: "You can tell what's wrong with *Crossroads* when you try to describe it to your friends. Halfway through the plot description, their eyes glaze over" and that's exactly what happens as you watch the film too. Essentially a mismatched buddy road movie (how original) with musical touches, the film follows two musicians from different sides of the tracks as they head down to Mississippi in search of a lost blues song. On the way they meet up with fellow hitcher Jami Gerz and have a series of semi-comic encounters with the locals *en* route. The film culminates with a totally ridiculous guitar duel between real-life musician Steve Vai and Macchio (who never once convinces as a great player and mimes throughout) at an otherwise all-black funeral. Go figure. It's hard to work out the point of it all, but if you like Cooder, it's just about worth watching to hear him play Macchio's numbers behind the scenes.

The ludicrous, violent drugs cartel thriller *Extreme Prejudice* (1987) returned Hill somewhere closer to home. It was based on a story by John Milius and, like *The Long Riders*, wears its influences on its sleeve with an explosive conclusion which echoes both *The Wild Bunch* and *Butch Cassidy and the Sundance Kid*. Nick Nolte stars as (what else?) a maverick Texas Ranger, alongside Powers Booth who plays his childhood-buddy-turned-nemesis Cash Bailey, a drug dealer from the other side of the river. Rip Torn is seen briefly as Nolte's partner, before getting blown away by the bad guys (including a rogue Black Ops army team intent on ripping off Cash's, um, cash).

To be honest, it's a bit of a mess (the studio didn't like it and forced Hill to make many cuts) but it's good to see *Scanners'* Michael Ironside as the Black Ops commander and Hill turning out another 18-certificate movie (the certification system in

the UK was overhauled in 1982, with the X certificate being replaced due to its connotations with explicit sex). Producers Carolco, formed by Lebanese Mario Kassar and Hungarian Andrew Vajna, were, at the time, developing a reputation for turning out high-concept action movies, including the *First Blood* films. The company would go on to fund Hill's *Red Heat* and *Johnny Handsome* and, in the '90s, made bucket loads with *Total Recall, Terminator 2* and *Basic Instinct* but were finally made bankrupt in 1995 by Renny Harlin's disastrous *Cutthroat Island* (which lost the studio millions).

Things to enjoy in *Extreme Prejudice* include the obvious western motifs: duels, showdowns and macho repartee (it's a movie in which everyone scowls, even the leading lady Maria Conchita Alonso, who has almost nothing else to do). William Forsythe hams things up enjoyably as a cigar chompin' bad guy, and the Mexican borderlands are effectively shot by cinematographer Matthew F. Leonetti, who had previously worked on, amongst others, Tobe Hooper's *Poltergeist* (1982), popular whodunit *Jagged Edge* and Arnold Schwarzenegger actioner *Commando* (both 1985).

Things to dislike are Jerry Goldsmith's dated synth drum heavy soundtrack, the misogynistic attitude towards its female characters (there's a fair degree of unnecessary nudity here which does nothing to further the narrative), and predictable plotting. Watched again recently, it's clear Hill was definitely losing his mojo by this point and even the action scenes are lacklustre (especially a sloppy car chase, which comes as a surprise from the man who directed *The Driver*).

Red Heat, which Hill directed in 1988, took advantage of the newly generated star power of Arnold Schwarzenegger (it was released just after 1987's *Predator* and *The Running*

Man and in the same year as the dreadful comedy *Twins* - which proved, unaccountably, to be far more popular than *Heat*) and, like *Extreme Prejudice*, is also notable for its 18 certificate. It's yet another (yawn) mismatched cops tale, with the twist being that one of them is a Russian. However, the teaming of Arnie and the slobby Jim Belushi (whose [blues] brother John had died of a lethal heroin and cocaine overdose in 1982) fails to capture *48 Hrs.'* spark. It's a reasonable time passer which tones down some (but not all) of the excesses of the action genre and is a little more character-driven (bizarrely Belushi is shown smoking on the movie poster and yet never lights up once in the actual film). However, like *Extreme Prejudice*, it all feels a little flat-footed. Peter Boyle is on-hand as the aggravated (is there any other kind?) police chief and the sultry Gina Gershon has a thankless role as the baddie's wife and gets bumped off early.

Arnie fans will no doubt enjoy his tastefully edited nude fight in the snow at the beginning. The film also features a pretty typical "Walter Hill smashes up the place with a bus" climax. There are minor roles for Hill regular Brion James as a pimp and bug-eyed Pruitt Taylor Vance as a seedy hotel lobby clerk plus, less predictably, a script which was re-drafted by none other than Troy Kennedy Martin (it was rewritten several times whilst production was underway and it shows). Probably the best thing about it are some great graphics in the opening credits which were

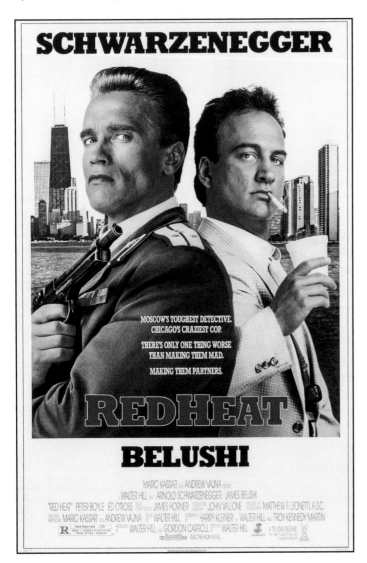

created by the prolific title designer Wayne Fitzgerald (whose work also includes, amongst others, *In the Heat of the Night, Bonnie and Clyde, The Graduate, Chinatown, One Flew over the Cuckoo's Nest, The Deer Hunter, Reds, Body Heat* and *Tootsie*).

The film is dedicated to its stunt co-ordinator Bennie Dobbins who died of a heart attack whilst working on location in Austria, aged 55. Dobbins had previously worked on both Hill's *Extreme Prejudice* and Arnie's *Commando* in 1985.

Like *Crossroads, Extreme Prejudice* and *Red Heat*, 1989's promising New Orleans-set *Johnny Handsome*, which featured '80s star *du jour* Mickey Rourke, also turned out to be a box office dud, quite possibly because of the rather odd decision to cover one of the decade's most attractive male stars in layers of prosthetics for a third of the running time. It's based on a novel by John Godey, who also wrote *The Taking of Pelham One Two Three*.

Elizabeth McGovern and Morgan Freeman also appear - as does Forest Whitaker in a minor role - and Lance Henriksen and a vicious, very big-haired Ellen Barkin play the particularly brutal villains. It's the downbeat (and rather silly) tale of the eponymous Johnny, a deformed, Elephant Man-like petty criminal, who receives facial reconfiguration surgery after he's arrested following a heist gone wrong (like you do). Now sporting a new look, he tracks done his former partners and wreaks his revenge. There's much smoking, gunplay and harsh language and it all ends fairly bleakly. Ry Cooder's back on soundtrack duties and, whilst this is certainly no masterpiece, it's another enjoyable time waster which reminds us that Hill was always happy keepin' 'em snappy: *Johnny Handsome* clocks in at a lean 89 minutes. Marvel Studios take note.

In the '90s, Hill's films continued to be interesting, if erratic: the inevitable sequel *Another 48 Hours* (1990) failed to capture the magic of the original; *Trespass* (1992) has its admirers; he also made two more low key westerns - 1993's *Geronimo* and 1995's *Wild Bill*. In 1996, he returned to the Depression era for his take on *Yojimbo*, the massive

flop *Last Man Standing*. To add insult to injury, Hill then got fired from the disastrous science fiction mess *Supernova* in 2000 (Francis Coppola was called into sort this one out, but failed miserably). After that, on the big screen, it was more or less silence.

However, the superb HBO TV series *Deadwood*, which Hill produced and occasionally directed, provided him with the opportunity to prove that there was life in the old dog yet. It remains a yardstick for the kind of quality American TV show we now take for granted.

Since the early 2000s, Hollywood has lost its penchant for turning out small-scale, intelligent thrillers made by interesting minor directors which clock in at the 90-minute mark. The American film industry no longer appears to nurture this type of film or filmmaker. Which is a great pity because, along the way, Hill made some of the most solid and enduring thrillers (and westerns) of the last 50 years and for that we should be extremely grateful. He may not have been as cool as some of his contemporaries, but he sure once knew (at least, before he foolishly decided to make his comeback low-budget western, the derivatively titled *Dead for a Dollar* in 2021) how to handle a shootout!

And, sometimes, that's just what us movie-goers need.

by Joseph Secrett

A curious film in the sense that its effects are of more interest than its stars, *Comin' At Ya!* is a late spaghetti western which helped revive the 3-D boom which had first found favour in the '50s. By the '80s, 3-D was long out of fashion and the spaghetti western sub-genre was pretty much dead too. Some belated greats had come out in the late '70s, but only a few minor footnotes had appeared in the early '80s (such as the 1981 comedy *Buddy Goes West*, one of Bud Spencer's last hurrahs in the genre). The simple fact was that there was barely an audience for them anymore. The once-bustling sets were left to crumble (in *Mannaja*'s case, shrouded with fog to simulate a mostly abandoned ghost town), and the directors, actors and writers had moved into crime films and giallos.

Enter actor, writer and producer Tony Anthony. He was no stranger to westerns, having starred in a series of them playing an aptly-named Eastwood knockoff, 'The Stranger'. The early entries in the series were quite successful albeit conventional. The fourth title, *Get Mean* (1975), took an extremely surreal turn, incorporating barbarians, a hunchback and magic into its outlandish storyline. The series was not continued.

In the '80s, Anthony teamed up with Ferdinando Baldi - with whom he'd worked previously on the *Zatoichi*-styled *Blindman* (1971) - and together they set out to try a unique approach to the western genre, utilising the 3-D concept.

The result was *Comin' At Ya!* (1981), which made a mark at the box office and saw those involved being credited with a brief revival of 3-D movies. The success of *Comin' At Ya!* led to a spate of other titles adopting the process, notably *Friday the 13th Part 3*, *Amityville 3-D*, *Parasite*, *Jaws 3* and *Silent Madness*.

H.H. Hart (Anthony) is getting married to his sweetheart Abilene (Victoria Abril) when the service is interrupted by the Thompson Brothers - Pike (Gene Quintano) and Polk (Ricardo Palacios) - who kill the priest, wound Hart and kidnap Abilene, intending to sell her (and many others) into slavery in Mexico. Fueled by anger, Hart arms himself with a pump-action shotgun, teams up with a Scottish preacher (Lewis Gordon), and races after the Thompson Brothers to rescue Abilene from a life of abuse south of the border. Bullets, flaming arrows, spears, coins and a baby's bare bottom are just some of the things *comin' at ya* during the course of the film. You can tell when a 3-D sequence is about to happen because most of the actors in the shot usually stare unnaturally at the camera. Many of the 3-D shots take place with the camera positioned at an exaggeratedly low angle. 3-D sequences are thrown our way every few minutes - cards are dealt into our face, flaming arrows narrowly avoid us, coins are dropped over the camera while various Italian western regulars laugh or grin evilly in the background. "The management is not responsible for where the screen ends and you begin!" quipped the Filmways poster for the American release.

The plot is by-the-book - there's nothing here you haven't seen before and it all fits the standard formula. How often have we watched a distraught lover pursue a path of vengeance? The slavery angle is a little less common in the western genre, though *Blindman* utilised a similar plot device with the titular hero (also played by Anthony) attempting to rescue fifty mail-order brides who have been kidnapped to be sold into slavery south of the border. Minus the blind hero, *Comin' At Ya!* has a lot in common with *Blindman*, albeit more graphically violent. It is packed with over-the-top action, but doesn't outstay its welcome.

It's not the kind of movie that should be taken seriously. The dialogue is cheesy and stilted at times, though thankfully there's not much of it (in an interview, Anthony claimed only 51 lines of dialogue are used during the whole feature). Nevertheless, the action and 3-D effects are pretty engaging for the time. There are blood squibs aplenty, with some nasty shotgun blasts and a brutal impaling benefitting from the 3-D technology. At one point, a poor thug stumbles toward the camera after being impaled by a pitchfork, a scene seemingly borrowed for a similar 'kill' in *Friday the 13th Part 3*.

Anthony's H.H. Hart is by no means a breath of fresh air in the genre. Like a thousand other western anti-heroes, he's quiet, growls most of his lines and looks mildly irritated for the duration (with everything that happens to the character, who can blame him?) That said, he has a certain everyman charm, much like he did in *The Stranger* series (where he was cunning but vulnerable, often finding himself humbled, beaten or tortured by the bad guys and forced to stoop to underhand tactics to outwit his foes). It's not completely unreasonable to look upon *Comin' At Ya!* as an unofficial fifth entry in *The Stranger* series. He even borrows some of the character's hide-and-seek gunplay tactics, like hiding under floorboards and blasting thugs in their nether regions as they step over him.

Lewis Gordon's Preacher character, who briefly works with Hart to locate the Thompsons brothers, provides the basic exposition and sets Hart off on his quest, only

to tag along with him. No-one will be surprised to find his character saddled with all the cliches of a typical sidekick, including an early departure before the final showdown. Gordon is quite lively in his role, his dialogue slipping between a slight American accent and a Scottish twang, and he seems to have the most lines during the brief 87-minute runtime. He puts in a very serviceable performance.

The Thompson Brothers, Pike and Polk (played, respectively, by producer Quintano and Euro western regular Palacios), are suitably brutal villainous types. Quintano only appeared in two films, and was more prolific behind the scenes as a writer and director (*Comin' At Ya!* and *Treasure of the Four Crowns* were his only acting gigs). Several spaghetti western regulars can be spotted by eagle-eyed viewers (the likes of Luis Barboo, Gofreddo Unger and Domencio Cianfriglia), and genre fans will get a kick out of seeing them in one of the last spaghettis ever made.

Carlo Savina's score is, dare I say, his career best. Some of the tracks are very mournful, well suited to the tone of the plot. Harmonicas are plentiful in establishing the mood, and there is some beautiful vocal work by Edda Dell'Orso.

Fernando Arribas' beautiful cinematography really enhances the film, with fantastic images of dusty, empty

ghost towns and wide desert landscapes. Aside from the 3D, some of the other visual effects - like the colour adjustments where certain scenes switch to black-and-white but the blood remains red - are quite unique and effective. *Sin City* (2005) would use this style for the whole feature, but here it is used sparingly, notably during the opening kidnap sequence when Hart is wounded by the brothers, as well as in a few minor scenes later on. Some of these were edited in recent releases for the standard 2-D edition.

Comin' At Ya! proved a modest success, prompting Anthony to make another 3-D film, this time an action-adventure about treasure hunters. Released in 1983, *Treasure of the Four Crowns* did not perform well at the box office and Anthony retired from acting, mainly serving as a producer on future projects.

Though it could be considered a minor footnote in the history of spaghetti westerns, *Comin' At Ya!* proved popular enough to revive the 3-D gimmick from nearly 30 years prior. The '80s 3-D craze was relatively short-lived, but at the time of writing it's in vogue once more, recent *Jurassic Park* reboots standing as a good example of more sophisticated 3-D technology being used. 3-D has some undeniable charm to it.

Mainstream audiences might be put off by *Comin' At Ya!*'s absurd levels of violence and its grotesque and sadistic content, but spaghetti fans will get a kick out of it. The film can be watched with or without 3-D (the current releases on DVD and Blu-ray offer both options). It's a niche film by today's standards, but as gimmicky cult westerns go, it is huge fun.

60

GREYSTOKE
THE LEGEND OF
TARZAN
LORD OF THE APES

A Unique and Impressive Interpretation

by David Flack

Let's not beat around the bush. *Greystoke: The Legend of Tarzan, Lord of the Apes* (1984) is a wonderful, astonishing film, particularly considering the time it was made. To this day, it is among my absolute favourites. I consider it excellent and over the next few pages will try to convey my love for it.

Edgar Rice Burroughs' character Tarzan has been portrayed in many films dating right back to the silent era of cinema. *Greystoke* was the forty-fifth film in the English language to feature the character. It's interesting to note he is never called Tarzan in this film; he is referred to alternately as John Clayton or The Earl of Greystoke. Essentially, this is what modern filmmakers might refer to as an 'origin story'.

French actor Christopher Lambert was, by my count, the seventeenth actor to portray the lord of the apes in this, his first English-language film. Among others considered for the role were Julian Sands, Viggo Mortensen and, reputedly, Richard Gere. I'm

delighted they went with Lambert, because he is excellent in the role and, for me, easily the best Tarzan ever depicted on screen. He leaves the others - including the much-loved Johnny Weissmuller - far behind. Absolutely no contest.

The plot depicts John Clayton (Paul Geoffrey) and his wife Alice (Cheryl Campbell) setting off for missionary life in Africa in the late 19th century but being shipwrecked along the way. They survive for ten months in the jungle, during which time Alice gives birth to a child whom they also name John. Alice dies from malaria soon after and later John is killed by an ape. The apes take pity on the young, helpless child. They recently lost a baby of their own in an accident, so they raise toddler John in their way of life. Many years later, an expedition finds the tree-house built by the Claytons and an explorer named Phillippe D'Arnot (Ian Holm) comes across the now-grown White Ape (played in adult form by Lambert). D'Arnot teaches him the ways of the white man, and eventually they return to Britain and civilisation. John is restored to his position of aristocracy and learns he will become the next Earl of Greystoke when the current earl, his grandfather (Ralph Richardson), dies. Alas, the 'human jungle' proves considerably more difficult for him to navigate than the wild jungle where he was raised by the apes.

The synopsis doesn't do the film justice. You have to see it and let its magic engulf you. The impressive pre-credits sequence brings to mind Stanley Kubrick's *2001: A Space Odyssey* (1968), with an ape wielding a stick in the air. In fact, the entire first segment of *Greystoke*, which deals with the raising of the child and his growth into a youth, is engrossing and impressive. I'd venture so far as to call it astonishing. These scenes could have so easily been farcical and false-looking like many earlier 'man-in-a-monkey-suit' offerings. Here, though, they are totally convincing thanks to the actors playing the apes and Rick Baker's marvellously realistic costumes and make-up. A few real chimps were used, but most of what we see comprises gymnasts, acrobats, dancers and mime actors recreating realistic ape movements. They are nothing short of amazing. Remember, this was shot in 1983, when CGI was virtually non-existent - what they achieve here is frankly mind-blowing. It must have been a long and complex process to get these scenes right, but the crew and director Hugh Hudson do a fantastic job.

We see John Clayton as a baby, a five-year old and a twelve-year old, experiencing both happiness and tragedy as his animal friends fall prey to natural predators and his adopted mother is killed by natives. Lambert appears as the adult version of the character 34 minutes into the film, and from then on gives a thoroughly magnetic, charismatic performance. He is never less than convincing, and, while not particularly musclebound, is suitably athletic and gives a charming and moving performance.

After the opening section, the rest is basically divided into three other segments. First, we are introduced to a British Museum expedition which comes across the tree-house and uncovers the fate of the Claytons. The expeditioners are wiped out by a sudden and brutal native attack and only the leader, a Belgian captain named Philippe D'Arnot (Holm), survives albeit badly wounded. He is found and nursed back to health by the ape man.

In the next section, the White Ape and D'Arnot form a close bond, with the Belgian explorer teaching his pupil the laws and ways of the civilised world. Meanwhile, the pupil protects his teacher from the many perils of the jungle.

Finally, in the last segment D'Arnot takes John to civilisation where a fabulous inheritance awaits. John meets his grandfather (Richardson, in a role offered to Sean Connery) and Jane Porter (Andie MacDowell, making her film debut) and they feel an instant attraction. All is well for a while, but John can never forget where and how he was raised and finds this new existence far from easy. His civilised/wild side are in constant conflict.

The movie's first half is necessarily brutal and violent, portraying jungle life and death with dispassionate harshness (enough so to concern the distributors). Later, when John meets D'Arnot, the story concentrates on their relationship. The film could have lost its way here, but it doesn't thanks to warm and convincing acting between Lambert and Holm. The second half, when John returns to civilisation, loses a lot of the violence but remains fascinating, enthralling, amusing and ultimately heartbreaking. Despite seeming to enjoy early success as he attempts to blend in to his new surroundings, and an instant bonding with his grandfather, John's wild side is never far away and he has difficulty accepting that his parents were humans not apes. The civilised world is completely alien to what he is used to, and he only seems happy when in the company of his eccentric grandfather and Jane. Everywhere else, he encounters arrogance, bigotry and cruelty which constantly angers and frustrates him, and makes him pine for his previous, straightforward life in the jungle. The film does not paint a flattering picture of upper-

class aristocratic life and it's no surprise John's frustrations, tensions and anger build. Then his beloved grandfather dies, and soon after he discovers that his adopted ape father is alive in captivity in London. John frees the ape and they go off playfully to a London park which causes a major public panic and results in his ape's death. This sends John into an unhappy state. He reverts to 'wild man' status and, despite worthy attempts by D'Arnot and Jane to entice him back to his stately life, they both eventually accept he should have the final say about his future. If he decides to return the jungle, they will abide by his choice.

That view is not shared by the Earl of Greystoke's aide, Sir Evelyn Blount (John Wells), who firmly believes John should be brought into line and become the next earl whether he likes it or not. There is a great, tense scene between them when John announces his decision to go back to his jungle home. Sir Evelyn angrily states: "You are the Earl of Greystoke" and John menacingly stares him down, making guttural sounds before replying: "Half of me is, and half of me is wild." The film ends the only way it can, with John returning to his jungle home, setting up the basis of all the Tarzan novels/films that followed.

I have praised Lambert's performance a few times over the course of this article but I'd like to add one more thing about it. That is to say (and I think this is the ultimate compliment) that is difficult to imagine anyone else in the role, as he pulls it off so superbly.

In fact, *Greystoke* is dotted with fine performances, especially Holm as D'Arnot. This version and *Tarzan of the Apes* (1918) - the first ever Tarzan film - are the only screen versions to include his character despite him featuring prominently in the 1912 novel. Sporting an accent which reminded me of Hercule Poirot, Holm really grabs the attention, especially in the scenes between him and Lambert which are enduring and believable, their trust in each other unwavering. The scene near the end of the film, where D'Arnot calls out Sir Evelyn over his selfish plan to keep the Earl of Greystoke in the country, is an example of top-class acting and delivery.

Ralph Richardson is also excellent in what would prove his last film. His scenes with Lambert are very well done and again show masterful acting. He died six months before film was released and was nominated for a posthumous Oscar (but did not win which is a pity). Allegedly, some of his on-screen eccentricities may not have been acting - there were stories of him turning up for work on his motorbike in his leathers and crash helmet with a white pet rat in his pocket!

MacDowell as Jane Porter made her debut here and certainly looks good, though her American South accent was deemed unacceptable and dubbed over by Glenn Close (ironically also an American, though better at pulling off a British accent). MacDowell, understandably unhappy about this, nevertheless acquits herself well. The final scenes between John and Jane are very moving - she obviously loves him and wants him to stay, but realises it's his decision and respects his choice because of her deep love for him.

The supporting cast is first rate with memorable roles

for Nigel Davenport, James Fox and David Suchet in particular. I cannot talk about the acting and leave out the amazing ape actors who perform miracles in making their parts believable - Peter Elliott, Aisa Berk, John Alexander and Christopher Beck, to name a few, all excel in extraordinary performances.

Director Hugh Hudson also does a splendid job, especially considering this was only his second time in the director's chair after *Chariots of Fire* (1981). He didn't have much luck after this film, with a run of box-office failures (*Revolution* [1985], for example) but his work is really impressive here.

Greystoke, especially in its first half, sticks to the novel quite closely. The second half jettisons the novel entirely, but I don't think that really matters. It gets the balance just right and makes for wondrous, compelling entertainment. I feel it is a unique and impressive interpretation of a well-known, oft-filmed character.

Greystoke has a reputation as something of a box-office failure, but the facts don't warrant this. It was made for just over $30 million (how much would it cost today?) and earned $45 million, so was in profit. There was talk of a sequel which never materialised and I think would have gone down the more familiar Tarzan story route (e.g. standard jungle action heroics).

I'd like to end my musings with a confession. When I finished during previous viewings. Tears ran down my cheeks. Who cries watching a Tarzan film?!? Well, I do apparently. But I'm not ashamed to admit it as I love this film so much.

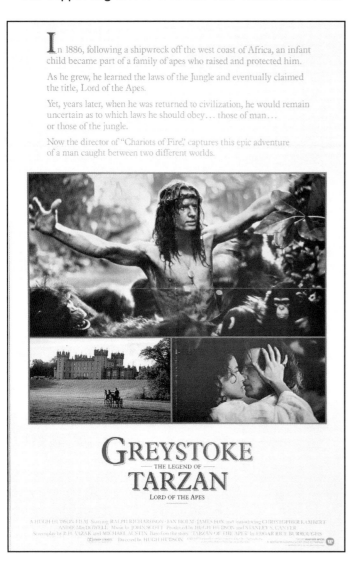

In 1886, following a shipwreck off the west coast of Africa, an infant child became part of a family of apes who raised and protected him.

As he grew, he learned the laws of the Jungle and eventually claimed the title, Lord of the Apes.

Yet, years later, when he was returned to civilization, he would remain uncertain as to which laws he should obey... those of man... or those of the jungle.

Now the director of "Chariots of Fire," captures this epic adventure of a man caught between two different worlds.

GREYSTOKE
— THE LEGEND OF —
TARZAN
LORD OF THE APES

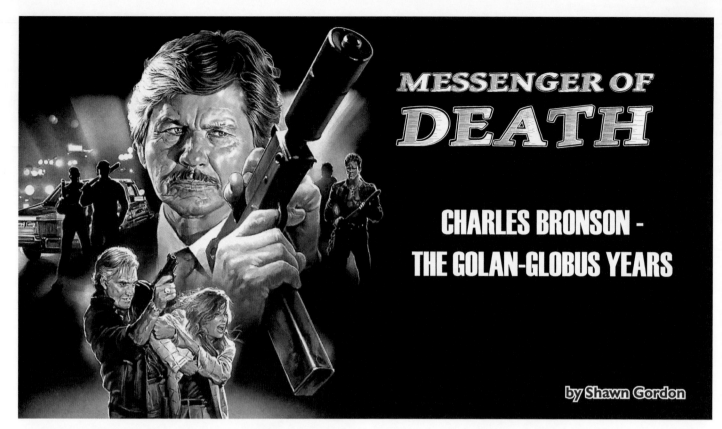

MESSENGER OF DEATH

CHARLES BRONSON - THE GOLAN-GLOBUS YEARS

by Shawn Gordon

Film historian David Del Valle, who worked as a script reader for the Cannon Group, said of Charles Bronson: "he was the jewel in the crown of action stars for Cannon Pictures." Indeed, Bronson was an icon of action before the genre went stratospheric. He helped pave the way for Cannon and similar companies to make a name for themselves releasing hyper-macho action pictures. His success was based on his unique screen image: a distinctive commanding voice, an incredible physique that he maintained until he was in his seventies, and, most importantly, knowing his audience and delivering what they wanted.

Bronson was one of the biggest international stars in the '70s but by the '80s was coming off a string of flops, including *The White Buffalo* (1977), *Love and Bullets* (1979), *Borderline* (1980), *Caboblanco* (1980) and *Death Hunt* (1981). He seemed to be having a difficult time transitioning to the '80s action movie aesthetic.

Producers Menaham Golan and Yoram Glous, two movie-loving cousins from Israel, had left a lucrative career in their own country to head to America to see if they could crack Hollywood. The cousins had purchased a struggling indie movie company called the Cannon Group for $50,000. Now, they were looking to make a significant splash on movie screens.

Bronson and the Go-Go Boys (Golan and Globus' nickname in the press) were ripe to cross paths. Both had something to prove and something to gain. The partnership they forged would play a key role in shaping the movie landscape of the decade.

The movies themselves would be obvious fare - eye for an eye, misogynistic, xenophobic and violent parables typical of the Regan era. They combined elements of classic film noir and macho action escapism with a dash of slasher-style thriller thrown in. In many ways, Bronson's contributions - a series of low-budget exploitation pictures - were indicative of the '80s action genre in general.

They were maligned by critics, who couldn't see past the low budgets, extreme violence, gratuitous nudity and semi-fascist attitudes. Bronson's Cannon movies were formulaic yet outlandish which, at the time, was enough to earn them an automatic fail grade from the intellectual elite. Yet their popularity has prevailed. Even now, four decades on, new generations are discovering these movies thanks to DVDs, Blu-rays, Netflix and other streaming services, appreciating and respecting them in ways that couldn't be imagined in the '80s. If nothing else, the internet age has done much to reduce the snobbery of years past.

The pictures were all produced by Pancho Kohner, son of Bronson's long time agent Paul Kohner. Most were directed by the British pair J. Lee Thompson and Michael Winner. Winner was Bronson's friend, having even dated Jill Ireland years earlier. The sometimes difficult star had a good working relationship with the director. They understood each other well, and Bronson appreciated his efficiency. Thompson was a former film editor who'd had early brushes with greatness on movies such as *North West Frontier* (1959), *The Guns of Navarone* (1961), *Cape Fear* (1962) and *MacKenna's Gold* (1969). He'd begun his directorial career in Britain with some pre-New Wave kitchen-sink dramas before receiving an Oscar nomination for *Guns of Navarone*. Despite working with huge budgets and major stars, his Hollywood career fizzled out abruptly at the end of the '60s. Thompson spent the majority of the '70s steadily descending into B-pictures, most below his talents though still worthwhile as popcorn entertainment. He was an expert at action and suspense, and the success of Bronson's movies at Cannon was in large part down to the talents of this underrated director.

Few of Bronson's Cannon movies really stood out at the time. The decade was awash with action pics, so it was a crowded field. Veteran tough guys like Bronson, Clint Eastwood, Burt Reynolds, Roy Scheider, Gene Hackman and younger guns like Sylvester Stallone, Bruce Willis, Arnold Schwarzenegger, Chuck Norris, Dolph Lundgren and Jean-Claude Van Damme were active in the genre. Several of them would even make entries for the Cannon Group. They rarely set the box office afire, but many became a staple of the VHS rental boom. Nowadays, '80s action films are celebrated with nostalgia and homaged in fare like the on-going *Expendables* franchise. It's no accident that these '80s offerings are almost never out-of-print and are not hard to find. They were once looked upon as the bastard offspring of their genre, but now they are a proud part of the heritage of action cinema.

Bronson's first project with Golan and Globus actually failed to get off the ground. *Death Sentence* would have been an adaptation by David Engelbach of Brian Garfield's novel of the same name, a direct sequel to *Death Wish*. The novel was set in Chicago six months after the events of *Death Wish*, with the character Paul Kersey continuing his vigilantism in the Windy City. He must face the consequences of his actions when he unintentionally spawns a copycat with less discriminating methods. A screen version would have been interesting and would have hopefully stayed close to its source material, exploring elements and themes that were lacking in the 1974 blockbuster.

Death Sentence was announced in 1981, with Menahem Golan lined up to direct and Hal Landers and Bobby Roberts serving as producers. Alas, it wasn't to be. A version starring Kevin Bacon finally limped out in 2007, but few people saw it and it differed greatly from its source, omitting all references to *Death Wish*.

Bronson's working relationship with Golan and Globus finally got underway with *Death Wish II* (1981), an official sequel to the 1974 blockbuster that had made Bronson a household name. It deviated significantly from the novel 'Death Sentence'.

Golan and Globus were so eager to produce a sequel to *Death Wish* that the duo announced plans to do so even before securing the rights. Golan likened *Death Wish* to *The Godfather* in the sense that it was a '70s movies of exceptional significance. Cannon finally purchased the rights from Dino De Laurentiis - a similar B-movie mogul

and producer of the '74 film - for $200,000.

David Engelbach, who had penned the unused adaptation of *Death Sentence*, wrote the screenplay. Winner was recruited to direct the sequel - the original *Death Wish* had been a launchpad for Bronson's Stateside career, but Winner had not prospered after that and hadn't had a single hit since.

Cast alongside Bronson was his wife, Jill Ireland. *Death Wish II* was filmed on location in Los Angeles in the 'scuzzy' parts of the city. Twenty off-duty police officers were hired as protection for the cast and crew. The Hollywood Hotel, abandoned and crumbling, was used as a filming location just before it was demolished. Shooting was swift and precise, with everyone trying to get their work finished before the commencement of a production and director's strike. It was a close-run thing - the strike occurred about two weeks after production wrapped.

The score was by Jimmy Page of Led Zepplin, providing one of the most distinctive and positive contributions to the movie. His guitar rock theme is a pleasure unto itself and massively enhances the movie. Page was Winner's neighbor, and the director asked him personally to score the film after deciding Golan and Globus' preferred choice - the *Shaft* Oscar-winner Issac Hayes - wasn't the right man for the job. It's hard to say what the outcome of Hayes' score would have been, but it probably would have

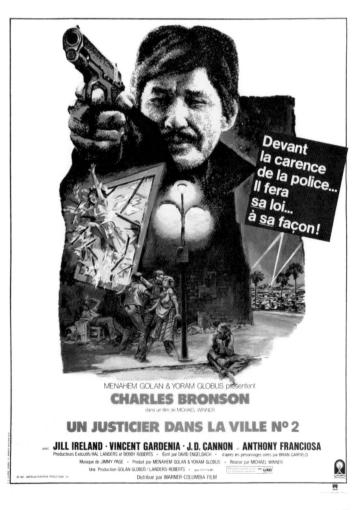

"DEATH WISH II"

"DEATH WISH II"

"DEATH WISH II"

"DEATH WISH II"

"DEATH WISH II"

had a more R&B-tinged urban vibe. Page's rock score fits the Bronson persona more strongly. Anyhow, the album soundtrack is nowadays rare and out-of-print and is a sought-after collector's item.

Death Wish II turned out to be Golan and Globus' most successful movie up to that point. It was a hit too on the newly established video rental scene. A fruitful partnership had begun.

Bronson's next movie with the Go-Go Boys was *10 to Midnight* (1983), an overt mixture of the slasher and revenge thriller genres. The two meld together well thanks to the knowing direction of J. Lee Thompson. Thompson was a dab hand at horror and suspense, having helmed such diverse fare as the classic 1962 thriller *Cape Fear* and the recent gore favourite *Happy Birthday to Me* (1981).

The script by director Thompson and William Roberts is better than average for this kind of movie. It was originally going to be titled *Bloody Sunday*, suggesting the intent was for a slasher pic rather than an action one. The screenplay uses psychology to create a real human explanation for the killer's murderous spree. He is motivated by sexual frustration

and, by making him cold, distant and creepy, the filmmakers keep the audience from feeling sympathy for him. Tight editing from the director's son Peter Lee enlivens the suspense. This was the first of several pictures he edited for his father.

Golan and Globus sold *10 to Midnight* at the Cannes Film Festival before they even had a story finalised. Producer Pancho Kohner came up with the movie's title, while Golan and Globus designed a poster that looked more like a straight action picture. They told potential investors the movie would be full of action,

danger and revenge.

The Evil That Men Do (1984) was pencilled in as a potential Golan-Globus production but things didn't work out and Lew Grade's ITC company ended up financing it. Next came *Death Wish 3*, which was

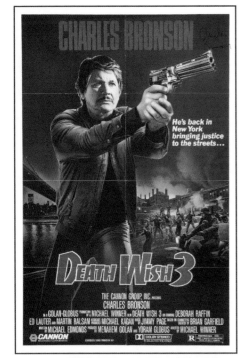

released at the end of 1985 and saw an increase in the level of cartoonish violence with Winner turning Paul Kersey into what he called "an urban Rambo." This entry moved away from the dark, noir-inspired tone of the previous movies to a lighter, almost comic-strip approach with an absurd body count.

Screenwriter Don Jakoby was more focused on penning science fiction screenplays for Golan and Globus including *Lifeforce* (1985) and *Invaders from Mars* (1986). This may explain why he chose to use the pseudonym Michael Edmonds for his work on *Death Wish 3*. Alas, Jakoby's script is pretty terrible and is one of the biggest factors in the movie's ultimate failure. The dialogue is almost unfathomable. The only saving grace is that it manages to become unintentionally comical as it progresses.

Much of the soundtrack music was recycled from the score provided by Jimmy Page for *Death Wish II*. *Death Wish 3* is poorly acted, with Bronson phoning in his performance while most of the young actors (including a pre-*Bill and Ted* Alex Winter) are amateurish at best.

Although set in New York, as was the 1974 original, *Death Wish 3* was filmed predominately in London. Cinematographer John Steiner did his best to hide the obvious English

locations, but this often left the movie feeling confined. The crew do what they can to hide the British locales, but it is overwhelmingly obvious that we are not in the Big Apple.

Although well-liked by fans and a box office hit (it even spawned a video game), *Death Wish 3* is the most problematic film in the franchise. It's not just that the production was marred by unconvincing locations and poorly filmed stunts, it also feels like this time Kersey is crossing a moral line. He seems to kill indiscriminately, blowing away young people simply because he doesn't seem to like them very much. When he deliberately provokes teenage gang members to steal his car stereo then proceeds to gun them down, Kersey has gone from anti-hero - an average Joe who is fed up and not gonna take it anymore - to a bona fide serial murderer. He even shoots characters in the back which seems symbolically unheroic.

Bronson was quite unhappy with *Death Wish 3*, not least because it shits all over the character and themes established in the earlier pictures by turning Paul Kersey into a one-man army. Bronson didn't care for the level of graphic violence, some of which was filmed when he was off-set. The whole production caused riffs between Bronson and Winner. After collaborating on-and-off for fourteen years, it marked the

end of their hitherto fruitful partnership.

The most memorable part of *Death Wish 3* has to be the Wildey .475 handgun that Bronson uses. It was his own personal handgun and it featured in most of the promotional artwork. Wildey Moore, the gun's creator, acted as a technical consultant and was pleased to see sales of his gun increase every time the movie aired on television.

Despite being such a cartoon, *Death Wish 3* arguably has more fans today than any other movie in the franchise. Silly as it is, it has become an unlikely cult classic, a guilty pleasure which people find enjoyable in spite of itself. It continues to serve as a gateway into the series and Bronson movies in general.

Bronson was next announced as the second lead in *The Delta Force* (1986), but the role ultimately went to Lee Marvin. Reports suggest Bronson dropped out because he didn't want to take second billing to the relatively new Chuck Norris.

His next movie for Cannon was *Murphy's Law*, released in the spring of 1986. Again, Bronson found himself starring in an urban action movie for J. Lee Thompson. This was becoming a familiar *modus operandi*. *Murphy's Law* is a very solid action vehicle for a number of reasons.

These Bronson movies were becoming increasingly in tune with the decade's predilection for violence, profanity and stylised action.

The actor plays a cantankerous alcoholic veteran LAPD detective, Jack Murphy, who likes to espouse the ill-tempered motto "don't fuck with Jack Murphy!" Murphy is framed for the murder of his ex-wife (Angel Tompkins) by an angry ex-con, Joan Freeman (Carrie Snodgress), who he put away years earlier. While in police custody, Murphy is handcuffed to a bratty teenage petty thief, Arabella McGee (Kathleen Wilhoite), who he'd arrested earlier for stealing his car. Together Murphy and Arabella escape and Murphy sets out to prove his innocence and apprehend Freeman.

The screenplay by Gail Morgan Hickman was well received by all at Cannon including Bronson. Hickman also received an associate producer credit. Bronson and the young writer formed a friendship that led to Hickman writing Bronson and Thompson's next collaboration for Golan-Globus, the fourth *Death Wish* entry.

Murphy's Law enjoys the distinction of being the only Bronson vehicle where the main antagonist is a woman. Snodgress was a moderately well-known actress who rose to prominence with her Oscar-nominated role in *Diary of*

a *Mad Housewife* (1970). She won a Golden Globe and a Golden Laurel for that film. She makes a memorable and compelling villain in *Murphy's Law*, a genuinely threatening adversary for Bronson and one of the most memorable baddies to grace a Cannon action pic.

It also marked the first of three Bronson Cannon movies where the score was at least partially composed by his stepson Valentine McCallum. In addition, Jill Ireland (Val's mother) is credited as a co-producer. Peter Lee once again provides some tight editing on one of his father's movies.

In some territories (including the US), Cannon distributed the HBO telefilm *Act of Vengeance* (1986). Although the title would lead one to expect another Bronson revenge picture, it was actually a change-of-pace dramatic film. He plays Jock Yablonski, a real-life coal miner's union leader who was assassinated in 1969. Bronson's co-stars include Oscar winner Ellen Burstyn (as his wife) and then-newcomers Ellen Barkin and Keanu Reeves. It also featured beloved character actor Wilford Brimley in his third and final movie with Bronson. Directed by John Mackenzie, *Act of Vengeance* was not a Golan-Globus production but I mention it here since Cannon did have a hand in its distribution.

His next proper Golan-Globus movie was *Assassination*, released in early 1987. It was directed by Peter Hunt, formerly a successful editor of action movies who had gone on to direct the sixth 007 film *On Her Majesty's Secret Service* (1969). Hunt was a very capable director who had already guided Bronson through one of his best starring roles in *Death Hunt* (1981) opposite fellow tough guy Lee Marvin.

Bronson's plays Jay Killian, a veteran Secret Service agent taken off the President's detail and put in charge of protecting the President's wife (Jill Ireland). He is obviously less than happy about this, but soon finds himself shielding her from assassins at every turn. Eventually warming to the First Lady, even finding himself charmed by her, he goes on the run with her to keep her safe.

Unfortunately, *Assassination* doesn't come close to Bronson and Hunt's previous collaboration in terms of quality. All the same, I still feel it is somewhat unfairly dismissed. It is a reasonably entertaining outing, less violent than most Cannon action pictures, but busy and suspenseful with a good sense of pace.

The movie marked the sixteenth screen collaboration between Bronson and Jill Ireland. The two had an

undeniable on-screen chemistry and it is a joy to watch them in their last screen appearance together (she succumbed to cancer in 1990).

Where *Assassination* suffers most is that the script is flimsy, often hackneyed and feels rushed. This is not necessarily the fault of writer Richard Sale, who'd also written Bronson's excellent supernatural western *The White Buffalo* (1977). It's more likely the result of Golan and Globus deciding to remove entire pages from the script to trim the budget. Sale was an extremely capable screenwriter and novelist whose credits include the classic presidential assassination thriller *Suddenly* (1954) starring Frank Sinatra. The full *Assassination* script would no doubt

have been well-rounded and more satisfying than the abridged version which made it to the screen.

Bronson's next movie, released in the fall of 1987, once more saw him portraying the vigilante Paul Kersey. *Death Wish 4: The Crackdown* marked a significant change for the series, with J. Lee Thompson replacing Michael Winner in the director's chair. It also had a different feel and approach compared with the earlier titles in the franchise.

Diverging further from the gritty wannabe realism of the first two movies, *Death Wish 4* embraces the macho one-man army theme introduced in the third film. It feels more in line with Cannon's popular Chuck Norris vehicles than earlier

Bronson outings. Gone are the youthful street punks; now Kersey sets his sights on adult villainy. *Death Wish 4* is all the better for it. The new direction takes the series deeper into the '80s milieu of action cinema. Under the direction of Thompson, the actor seems more at ease than in the previous movie.

In a plot reminisce of Akira Kurosawa's *Yojimbo* (1961), the story finds Kersey going after drug kingpins

when his girlfriend's daughter accidentally overdoses. Working on the behalf of a millionaire businessman (John P. Ryan) who also lost a loved one to drugs, Kersey is supplied with all the weaponry he needs to get the job done. However, once finished, he learns he's been duped and has been working all along as a pawn. He's been played into eliminating one drug lord's competition.

The picture saw Bronson working once more with screenwriter Gail Morgan Hickman. Hickman wrote three different scripts for the movie, but found himself rewriting pages on a daily basis even when filming was underway. Hickman originally envisioned a more cerebral film that ignored the third movie altogether and was a direct sequel to the second part. However, this was nixed by Golan and Globus who wanted "a mindless action movie." There is very little of the original intent left in the final film, though Hickman's homaging of *Yojimbo* and *A Fistful of Dollars* can still be seen.

Death Wish 4 would prove the lowest grossing *Death Wish* film at the domestic box office to that point. It was apparent Bronson no longer had the box-office muscle he once carried. He was still popular overseas and on the booming video rental market, though. Despite its mediocre theatrical performance, *Death Wish 4* was the most popular of the franchise on VHS.

Messenger of Death (1988) saw Bronson making a further attempt at transgression. This time he didn't play a cop or vigilante. In fact, the whole movie diverts away, at least temporarily, from the action genre. Alas, what could have been a new leaf for the aging star proved to be his biggest misfire for the Cannon Group.

Bronson stars as Garret Smith, a crime reporter for the 'Denver Tribune', who, while covering the massacre of a Mormon family, finds himself drawn into the mystery.

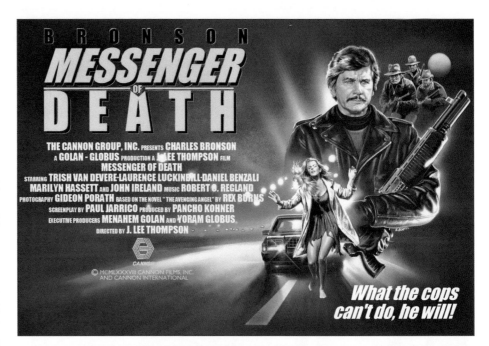

What the cops can't do, he will!

Believing religious motives are behind the heinous crime, Garret finds his story leading in different directions with the warring Mormon elders seemingly at the center of it all.

A thriller that fails to thrill, *Messenger of Death* moves at a lumbering pace with only the charisma of Bronson to carry it. The aging tough guy does his best, but he too seems bored by the material and gives one of his most sedate performances. At least he is assisted by a good supporting cast, including veteran western actors John Ireland, Jeff Corey and Charles Dierkop as well as Trish Van Devere (in the sort of role usually set aside for Jill Ireland).

Director J. Lee Thompson became ill during the shoot and had to turn

the film over to his second unit director Robert C. Ortwin. This may explain why the movie lacks Thompson's usual flair for suspense. Even the editing by the director's son Peter Lee could have been tighter to help it move along. It was the least successful, financially and creatively, of Bronson's collaborations with J. Lee Thompson for the Cannon Group.

Now 67 years of age, Bronson's next film would mark a return to blood-and-thunder action fare. *Kinjite: Forbidden Subjects* (1989) found the star back in familiar territory for his last movie for Golan and Globus. The Go-Go Boys were having financial troubles that would soon see Menaham leaving the company

he'd helped build. *Kinjite* would also be the last of nine collaborations between the star and director Thompson, as well as being his tenth and final teaming with producer Pancho Kohner. Despite all that, *Kinjite* is not a somber or reflective film. It represents a good, gritty, violent end to the decade for the star.

Starring as an LAPD vice-squad detective, Bronson brings years of gruff tough guy experience to his portrayal of Lt. Crowe. Older, sober and serious, but never subdued, Crowe is determined to bring down sleazy pimp Duke (Juan Fernandez), who preys upon teenage girls. Crowe also finds himself investigating the kidnapping of a Japanese businessman's (James Pax) teenage daughter (Marion Kodama), at first unaware that the two cases are connected.

Appearing in full-blown *Dirty Harry* mode, the elderly action star enjoys a lot of physically demanding violent scenes in *Kinjite*. He never looks like a senior citizen and remains a picture of brute force in his last big-screen hurrah for Cannon, at one point sodomising a bad guy with a dildo (off-screen) and at another forcing a villain to swallow his own wristwatch.

Following *Kinjite: Forbidden Subjects*, Bronson still owed two pictures to Cannon. But the company no longer existed in its original form. Menahem Golan had launched a post-Cannon company called 21st Century Films, and Bronson was roped in for one final *Death Wish* entry for them.

Death Wish V: The Face of Death was released in early 1994 and originally planned as a direct-to-video movie. As a '90s movie, it doesn't really belong in this magazine, but it seems worth mentioning for completion's sake. It managed a brief theatrical run in the U.S. but its box office performance was so poor that it might as well have gone straight to tape. It suffered from an obvious lack of finance, not to mention finesse, with action scenes downgraded from the previous entries to the level of the TV movies Bronson was starring in around the time. The Canadian locations were not remotely convincing, even worse than the British locales for Part 3. Sadly, the movie would be Bronson's final theatrical release, a poor send-off for the iconic tough guy.

Golan had proposed another *Death Wish* sequel, to be titled *The New Vigilante*. Allan A. Goldstein (who'd helmed *Death Wish V*) was attached to direct and it's likely the film would have been made without the participation of Bronson. Almost certainly destined to be a straight-to-video pic, the project died when Golan's 21st Century Films collapsed. Thus ended the story once and for all. Bronson died in 2003, Golan passed away in 2014 and Globus (at the time of writing) remains alive. Their collaborations in the '80s remain fascinating, enjoyable and still-popular examples from the boom era of the action genre.

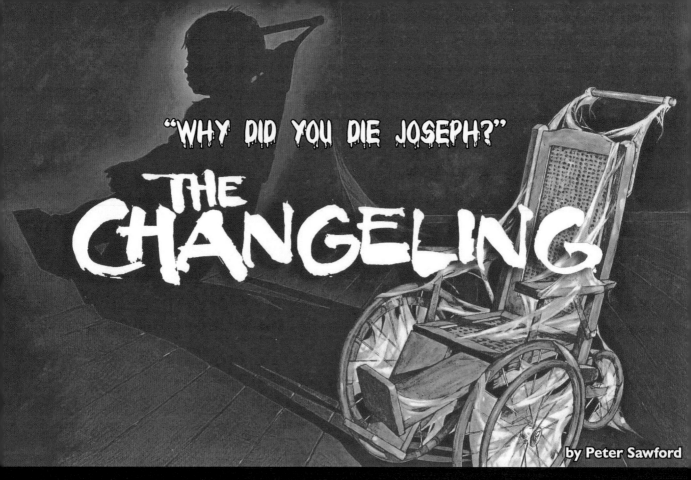

"WHY DID YOU DIE JOSEPH?"

THE CHANGELING

by Peter Sawford

During the late '70s and early '80s, horror films took a sharp left turn and moved away from the chills and suspense of previous decades. They began prioritising shock and gore in franchises like *Halloween*, *Friday the 13th* and *A Nightmare on Elm Street*. But one film bucked the trend and relied on good, old-fashioned, slow-burning story-telling to deliver its scares. The film in question was a throwback to that trusty old staple of filmic horror, the haunted house.

Released in 1980, *The Changeling* stars George C. Scott as John Russell a composer who, after seeing his wife and daughter killed in a car accident, moves to Seattle to restart his life. He rents a house from Claire Norman (Trish Van Devere), an agent of the local historical society, and soon afterwards begins to realise he's not alone within its walls. His 'guest' is not of this world, and everything that goes bump in the night eventually leads John to a senator named Joseph Carmichael (Melvyn Douglas) who is hiding a long-ago wrong that needs to be righted.

The screenplay, written by William Gray and Diana Maddox, was based on a story by Russell Hunter. Twelve years earlier, when Hunter was living in a mansion in Denver, Colorado, he had experienced strange paranormal events which led to the discovery of a body on the premises. Although only given a 'story by' credit, Hunter actually had a hand in co-writing the script and incorporated into t many of the events that had happened to him in Denver

A Canadian production, the film was produced by Garth Drabinsky and Joel Michaels. It also marked the first time Mario Kassar and Andrew G. Vajna were credited as executive producers on a picture. They would later go on to form Carolco Pictures, the company behind blockbusters such as *Rambo*, *Total Recall* and *Basic Instinct* in the late '80s and early '90s.

Tasked with helming the film was Hungarian born Peter Medak whose previous credits included *A Day in the Life of Joe Egg* and *The Ruling Class* (both 1972). Medak fully embraces the tradition of the genre, using every tool possible to heighten tension and send chills down the audience's spine as he gently turns the screw and ups the ante. Ethereal visions float across the screen, doors quietly open by themselves, staff appear seemingly out of nowhere, and the camera wanders silently around the rooms and halls, constantly keeping viewers on their toes and at the edge of their seats.

Throughout, Medak uses inanimate objects to express a sense of threat and to scare. Objects fly across the room, a tin bath suddenly opens a window to past events, a discarded rubber ball reappears from nowhere, and so on. I never imagined, for example, that a stationary old wheelchair could send such a tingle down your spine and convey such a sense of dread.

The anxiety levels are increased when Russell starts to be woken by a loud banging noise at the same time every morning. Shortly afterwards, he discovers a long-abandoned room at the top of a blocked-off flight of stairs, further increasing his curiosity. Medak really kicks the film up a notch when, after seeing an apparition and discussing the situation with Claire, Russell decides to hold a séance to unearth what is happening. He records the proceedings, and when he plays back the recording he hears the ghostly voice of the entity and finally begins to understand that someone - or something - from the house's past is trying to contact him. He realises the spectre isn't trying to scare him like he first thought; rather, it needs his help to finally be at peace.

After the séance, Russell's investigations attract the attention of Senator Carmichael, who has vested interests in past events at the house and plans an intervention to derail Russell's enquiries. Carmichael, a veteran of the political world, begins with gentle warnings and subtle threats but, when these fail, resorts to more direct and malicious actions. This leads to the film's only slight misstep, a scene involving a character who meets an early and violent death well away from the house (the entity has never shown any ability to influence events or people away from the premises).

With the information from the séance, Russell and Claire dig deeper into the history of the house. They eventually make a discovery which answers their questions but brings to light a murder, a cover-up, and a potential political scandal.

Van Devere is wonderful as the letting agent who is sceptical at first but gradually begins to realise there's something in the property that shouldn't be there. Her willingness to help Russell uncover the truth threatens to cost her her job at the historical society and potentially her life but she presses ahead regardless. The look of terror on her face in one scene makes the hairs on the back of our neck stand on end, even before we see what's scaring her! She was married to Scott in real life, and this adds to their on-screen chemistry as the relationship between their characters blossoms and grows.

Born in 1901, Douglas was one of the greats of cinema. He was perhaps most famous as the man who finally breaks the icy exterior of Greta Garbo in *Ninotchka* (1939). The year before *The Changeling*, he'd won a belated Best Supporting Actor Oscar for playing Benjamin Rand in Hal Ashby's *Being There*. Here he proves that his brilliance in that film was no last flash in the pan. In one of his last screen appearances, Douglas plays the senator who knows the long-held secret of the house and does everything in his power to stop Russell digging into the past and tearing down everything he's fought to build. Douglas draws upon his experience from a career spanning nearly 50 years to make the senator a vulnerable and sympathetic character with a core of steel - a man not afraid to abuse his power and position to get what he wants.

Jean Marsh makes a blink-and-you'll-miss-it appearance as Russell's doomed wife whose life is snuffed out at the beginning of the film. Barry Morse has an equally brief role as a doctor whom Russell turns to for possible answers. Overall, though, Scott's performance drives the film and is central to almost every scene.

An actor of huge range and experience, he had enjoyed a long and impressive film career before appearing in *The Changeling*. Notable performances included *Anatomy of a Murder* (1959), *Dr. Strangelove* (1964) and *Patton* (1970), the latter notable as the role for which he won then refused a Best Actor Oscar. Despite his prowess as an actor, his performance in the early stages of *The Changeling* doesn't seem quite right. The various paranormal events taking place around him seem to illicit no reaction - some semblance of surprise, shock or fear would seem in order. A window smashes from the inside and the glass nearly hits him as he's walking away, but he doesn't flinch or show any shock. He treats the occurrence as if it's of no consequence at all. You start to get the feeling that he's phoning his performance in. Audiences need an outlet for their own fears and dreads. It important that the characters on screen give vent to those fears. Van Devere does this in spades, but Scott barely behaves like anything untoward is happening during the first half of the movie. It's only after the séance scene that he starts to react, and at that point you realise his performance is actually extremely well judged and brilliantly nuanced. He's so distraught over the recent loss of his wife and daughter that he's lost in a fog of grief and despair, numb with shock and grief. The death of his beloved daughter is proving particularly hard for him to come to terms with. The rest of the world is passing him by in a daze. Even the extraordinary supernatural events happening around him are not powerful enough to penetrate the cocoon of sadness he's wrapped himself in. Only when he plays back the recording of the seance is he finally jarred back into the real world. Medak was smart enough to let Scott follow his instincts and play the role in this initially detached manner, never trying to bring the actor out of his shell until he felt the time was right.

The Changeling provided Canadian composer Rick Wilkins with his first major film score. Melancholic and sad one moment, eerie and unnerving the next, his score compliments the scenes superbly. A nice creepy touch is when a music box plays the same music that Russell is composing at his piano.

Dutch born Cinematographer John Coquillon, whose previous credits included a trio of Sam Peckinpah films (*Straw Dogs*, *Pat Garrett & Billy the Kid* and *Cross of Iron*), never lets the camera intrude and doesn't revert to rote camera tricks when a simple straightforward shooting style is all that's needed. He deservedly won a Canadian Academy of Cinema and Television Award (known as a 'Genie') for his work on *The Changeling*.

Released in March 1980, the film was a commercial and critical success and soon achieved cult status. Often the 'cult' label is given to films that didn't set the world on fire upon release, but over time gathered a loyal following. In this case, the movie was positively received from day one.

The Changeling is a real throwback to the heyday of horror films, the kind which make you grip the edge of the seat and jump at every sudden noise. Movies like this would stick with you on the journey home from the cinema, often fuelling your nightmares hours later.

Why did Joseph have to die? *The Changeling* will give you the answers… but don't expect a peaceful night's sleep afterwards!

RUNAWAY TRAIN

by Dawn Dabell

"The Cannon Group, Inc. Presents... A Golan-Globus Production." These words appeared in the opening credits of many a movie during the '80s. Menahem Golan and Yoram Globus were a pair of enthusiastic Israeli cousins who took charge of the Cannon production company in 1979, rescuing it from financial ruin, and began churning out movies at an impossible rate. Many of their releases followed a tried and trusted schlock/exploitation formula, with stars like Charles Bronson and Chuck Norris headlining action fare like *Death Wish II, III* and *IV, 10 to Midnight, Murphy's Law, Missing in Action, Invasion USA* and *Firewalker*. Every now and then, though, the "Bad News Jews" (as Menahem and Yoram were nicknamed) would produce something completely unexpected and un-Cannon-like. *That Championship Season* (1982) is one such example, a character drama based on an award-winning play, featuring a knockout cast that included Martin Sheen, Robert Mitchum, Paul Sorvino, Bruce Dern and Stacy Keach. Another is *Duet for One* (1986) with Julie Andrews, Alan Bates and Max Von Sydow, about a talented concert violinist whose career is cut short by multiple sclerosis. They even funded Jean-Luc Godard's French new wave-flavoured version of *King Lear* (1987) with eclectic names

like Norman Mailer, Burgess Meredith and Woody Allen among its cast.

Another example, one of the best and most unheralded films of the decade, is *Runaway Train* (1985). While this one does fit in the action genre to an extent, and is thus loosely aligned with the standard Golan-Globus product, it is so unconventionally plotted and offers such fascinatingly off-kilter characters and unique visuals that it emerges another extremely un-Cannon-like Cannon film.

It was originally conceived in the '60s by Japanese director Akira Kurosawa, who envisaged it as an American-set drama to be shot in upstate New York. His idea centred on a pair of escaped convicts - he had Henry Fonda and Peter Falk in mind - who hide from their pursuers on a train, but the train ends up hurtling down the track out of control and driverless. Kurosawa planned to set it in winter and wanted to shoot in colour, but the potential financers felt colour photography was a waste of money - a big, black train careening through a white, snowy landscape ought, they felt, to be shot using the cheaper black-and-white process. Unable to drum up sufficient interest or money, Kurosawa dropped the idea and moved onto other things.

The original, unpolished Kurosawa script sat gathering

dust for the best part of two decades in the vault of the Nippon Herald company. In he '80s, Francis Ford Coppola was asked if he could think of a director who might be able to revive the script and turn it into a film. Coppola nominated the Russian director Andrei Konchalovsky, who had enjoyed success in his native land and had been looking to get a break in the American film market. Konchalovsky sought financial backing from the Israeli producers at Cannon, and was excited when they granted him the go-ahead to modernise it and turn it into an action-drama for contemporary audiences. It would be Konchalovsky's first English-language picture.

The Russian filmmaker was on friendly terms with American star Jon Voight. The pair had combined their energies to attempt to get a movie off the ground called *Rhinestone Heights* in 1979, but had been unable to make it happen. Voight was a big champion of the director's Russian work and had been vocal in making western audiences aware and appreciative of such films as *The First Teacher* (1964) and *Siberiade* (1979). He'd also helped Konchalovsky obtain his visa to work in the United States.

Given virtual carte blanche by Golan and Globus (their sole proviso being that he needed to keep within the budget), Konchalovsky was determined to turn *Runaway Train* into something unique and special. It was his chance to make a real mark on the American movie scene and he was desperate to do himself proud. He sent the script to his pal Voight and asked him to play the lead, a savage and animalistic life-term convict named Oscar 'Manny' Manheim. Initially Voight was reluctant to accept the role. He found aspects of the script lacking and wanted parts rewriting; he also didn't think he was right for such a hardened brute of a character, seeing himself as more of a blond-haired, blue-eyed, all-American good guy. He eventually came round to Konchalovsky's way of thinking, not only accepting the role but turning it into one of the best of his career, with an Oscar nomination to show for it.

The plot sticks to the fundamental concept of Kurosawa's script, but adds language, violence and grit more in keeping with the '80s action landscape. Two convicts - Manny (Voight), a savage lifer feared and idolised by his fellow inmates, and Buck (Eric Roberts), a well-built simpleton doing time for statutory rape - bust out of Stonehaven, a remote maximum security jail in Alaska. Braving sub-zero temperatures and the pursuing manhunt, they somehow make it to a railyard where they board a passing freight express.

Their luck is about to change for the worse, though, because during a routine manoeuvre in the yard the train engineer suffers a fatal heart attack and falls from the vehicle. With the throttle wide open and the brakes burned through, the train is soon hurtling at terrifying speed across the Alaskan wilderness. It takes a while

Eric Roberts by Aaron Stielstra

before stowaways Manny and Buck even realise there is a problem. The only other person on the train is the hostler Sara (Rebecca DeMornay), who is initially terrified of the two desperadoes and tries to explain to them there is no way of stopping the train since the lead engine cannot be reached. Their only hope is to uncouple the engine car from the rest of the express, an incredibly dangerous, almost impossible feat at the speed they are travelling.

With the maniacal prison warden Rankin (John P. Ryan) desperate to catch his escaped convicts, and the team at the railroad computer centre - headed by Frank Barstow (Kyle T. Heffner) - looking on with panic and alarm as the crisis unfolds, it seems inevitable the train will thunder its way to destructive doom.

It's extraordinary to think very little of the shoot took place on a moving train. The vast, bleak Alaskan wilderness and the speeding train seem vividly real throughout, yet most of the interiors were shot on a mock-up in a studio in California. The back projection looks remarkably real, with second unit photography seamlessly incorporated to give the impression of a train hurtling across the snowy wilds. Exterior lensing was supposed to be carried out in Montana, but when the team arrived they found the state basking in unseasonably warm weather for the time of year and what little snow was on the ground soon melted completely. They were forced to go to Alaska itself, where the story was set, to capture the required footage. But most of the film was shot in the studio and it's extraordinary how convinced we are that the actors are out there in the frozen wilderness. There are other neat visual tricks too - one sequence in which Voight's fingers are mangled in the couplings between two of the cars looks so real and authentically gruesome you can virtually feel his pain emanating from the screen. Alan Hume, who was better known around that time for working on the 007 films, does extraordinary work in the cinematography department.

Interestingly, the film makes the train itself as much

a character as the humans. In certain scenes, it almost seems to have a blackened face, twisted and furious, as it zooms along. The initial idea was to title the film *The Beast*, neatly tying together the fact that the express and Manny (and to some extent Rankin too) are all beasts in their own way. Somewhere along the line (pardon the pun), it was changed to *Runaway Train*. I think both titles have merit.

Voight's performance is mesmerising. We first meet Manny doing push-ups in his cell, having been welded in for the past three years on the orders of the warden. Following a protest by human rights activists, Rankin is ordered to move Manny back into general population. There's a savage intentness, a fearless edge to Manny which burns through every scene. During a boxing bout put on for the entertainment of the convicts, one of the prisoners attempts to kill Manny with a knife. Manny is stabbed through the arm and the hand, but still comes at his attacker without fear or mercy, blood pouring from his wounds almost unnoticed as he stalks towards the terrified would-be assassin. In his way, Manny is as unstoppable as the train itself. The voice, the make-up (ugly scars and crooked teeth) and the mannerisms all combine to make him seem unimaginably dangerous. There's a scene in which Manny delivers a powerful monologue, partly written and partly ad-libbed by Voight himself, which is just stunning. Both Konchalovsky and Roberts claimed they experienced goosebumps watching him perform this scene. His Oscar

nomination and Golden Globe win were richly deserved.

Also Oscar-nominated was Roberts as Manny's fellow escapee. The actor was initially puzzled how to play the role - he somehow needed to make a convicted rapist likable and identifiable. It was his own idea to change the character's accent and manner of speech, giving him a "country bumpkin" flavour which somehow lessened his unsavouriness and lent him a sympathetic vibe. He's like a big, dumb child - a 'Lenny' to Manny's 'George' to draw parallels with 'Of Mice and Men' - and we feel enormous pity for him when Manny convinces him to attempt a life-threatening clamber to the lead engine and kicks the hell out of him when he comes back unsuccessful.

There aren't any bad performances here. DeMornay is great as the grubby, spirited hostler (in a role offered to Karen Allen and coveted by Jodie Foster) and Ryan oozes a psychotic arrogance as the warden. A special mention to Eddie Bunker, an actor and real-life ex-con, who plays Manny's best friend on the inside. Bunker was asked to contribute to the script because his knowledge of how real prisoners act and speak was considered invaluable.

It's a great shame that *Runaway Train* was not a sizable box-office hit. One of the problems with Golan and Globus, indeed the thing which eventually brought the Cannon Group, Inc. to its knees, was the fact they didn't have a sensible marketing strategy for their products. Some of their movies succeeded on the strength of a popular star or positive word of mouth, others found an audience thanks to the boom in the video rental scene at the time. But the Israeli cousins themselves didn't have a particularly strong business model when it came to promoting their releases. It was almost like they financed and released as many pics as they could within a calendar year, regardless of how far into debt they might fall, and just kept their fingers and toes crossed for good returns. The philosophy seemed to be "if we make a load of films and release them in a load of cinemas, hopefully at least a couple will score a bullseye with the public."

Runaway Train was hailed as a work of real energy and power by most contemporary critics, yet it did only moderate business at the box office. Over the years, it has been rediscovered and praised as the exhilarating action-drama it is by viewers who missed it first time around. It's one of my favourite films of 1985, one that I can watch again and again without losing interest, spotting new details each time, and is, I believe, a contender for the finest movie Cannon ever released.

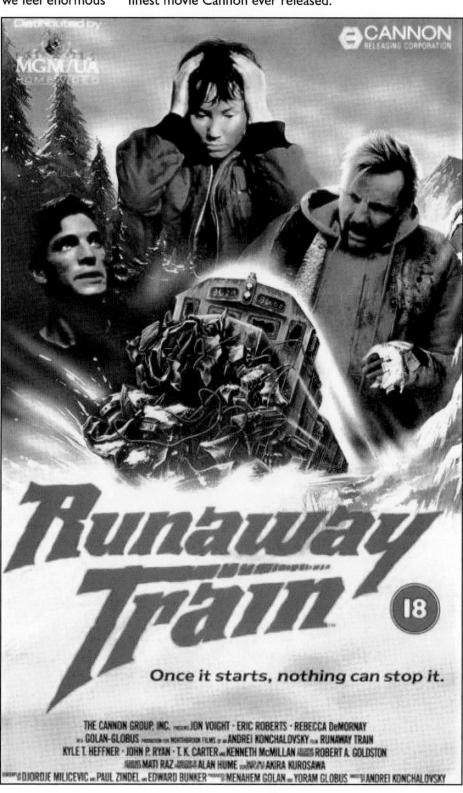

THE ADVENTURES OF BUCKAROO BANZAI

Across the 8th Dimension... and into the 21st Century!

by James Aaron

The '80s saw a cornucopia of influential science fiction films, and some of the most well-known skewed towards a darker end of the spectrum in terms of both style and subject matter. Many of the decade's greatest hits filled cinema screens with an almost dystopian cynicism: *Scanners, Blade Runner, The Thing, The Terminator, Brazil, Aliens, The Fly* and *Robocop* all saw the world through a definitively pessimistic view about the future of humanity.

But not all the era's most enduring sci-fi films fit the downbeat bill. In fact, perhaps the biggest cult success of the decade is also the sunniest. A bizarre but thoroughly entertaining concoction, *The Adventures of Buckaroo Banzai Across the 8th Dimension* danced between genres like few films ever have, before or since it hit theaters in August of 1984. Directed by W.D. Richter and written by Earl Mac Rauch, the film crosses genre boundaries with abandon: science fiction, comedy, action-adventure, romance and rock 'n' roll musical, all masterfully blended and balanced, and powered by a pair of hyper-magnetic performances from its two leading actors.

The plot may seem bewildering initially. Buckaroo Banzai, portrayed with charismatic intensity by Peter Weller, isn't your average action hero: he's that rare (to say the least) combination of neurosurgeon, test pilot, physicist and rock band frontman. In a breathtaking experiment, he drives a jet car straight through a mountain, utilizing the quantum-tunneling (just go with it) invention the Oscillation Overthruster. But in an unintended consequence, he inadvertently breaches into the 8th Dimension and opens up Earth to the threat of invasion by the Red Lectroids, extraterrestrials from Planet 10. To complicate matters, there's the villainous Dr. Emilio Lizardo, played with eccentric, scenery-chewing perfection by John Lithgow. Initially a brilliant physicist, Lizardo becomes possessed by a Red Lectroid during a failed Overthruster experiment of his own, turning him into an agent of chaos. With the stakes higher than ever, Buckaroo and his dynamic crew, the Hong Kong Cavaliers, must thwart the nefarious scheme of these alien invaders.

Those are the plotline skeleton on which hangs *The Adventure of Buckaroo Banzai*. From there, the story rips through its action and intrigue with a maniacal glee that I won't spoil here on the off chance that anyone reading this article hasn't actually seen the movie yet.

Still, there is plenty we can discuss.

For starters, any true discussion of *Buckaroo Banzai* must begin with an appreciation of its cast, which is buttressed by the strong support of luminaries like Christopher Lloyd, Jeff Goldblum, Ellen Barkin, Vincent Schiavelli, Clancy Brown and Dan Hedaya. These are all names that are well-recognized some four decades later thanks to their appearances in the credits of countless Hollywood classics. Jamie Lee Curtis also appeared as Buckaroo's mother in an alternate opening that was ultimately cut, but is widely available on home video, starting with the initial DVD release.

But even above the stellar supporting cast, the true strength of *Buckaroo Banzai* finds its anchor in the twin tour de force acting clinics turned in by Weller as the polymath hero and Lithgow as the supercharged, bounce-off-the-walls maniacal villain.

Today, Weller has a well-deserved reputation as one of sci-fi's heavyweight leading men in the '80s and '90s. In addition to *Buckaroo Banzai* and *Of Unknown Origin* (1983), he starred in the underwater monster movie *Leviathan* (1989), David Cronenberg's 1991 film version of the William S. Burroughs novel *Naked Lunch*, and the Philip K Dick adaptation *Screamers* (1995). And of course, he is best remembered today as the iconic title character in the stone-cold classic *Robocop* (1987) and its 1990 sequel. But at the time he was cast as Buckaroo Banzai, Weller had played mostly smaller dramatic roles in films like *Shoot the Moon* and *Butch and Sundance: The Early Days* and scattered television work. *Buckaroo Banzai* really gave him his breakthrough.

As Buckaroo, Weller showed a deft ability to be both earnest and whimsical. This unique blend has been appreciated by many critics and fans alike, with some pointing out that Weller's understated approach served as the perfect counterpoint to the many eccentricities of the film's breakneck plot, making the unbelievable seem entirely plausible. It could also be argued that Buckaroo is imbued with Weller's own sense of intellectual curiosity, which breathed even more life into the character. In real life, the actor would go on to gain a doctorate of his own, earning a PhD in Italian Renaissance art history, and is now an art historian in his own right.

Counterpoint to Weller's clinical levelheadedness is Lithgow's wild, extravagantly theatrical masterstroke as Dr. Emilio Lizardo/Lord John Whorfin. It was Lithgow who actually brought the most glittering Hollywood bona fides to the show, having been nominated for an Academy Award for his supporting role alongside Robin Williams and Glenn Close in 1982's *The World According to Garp*, and he certainly proved up to the task of playing an alien from another dimension. If Weller's intellectual protagonist has one foot in the clinical hospital at all times, Lithgow plays Lizardo as if he lives with one foot in the insane asylum (maybe more than one foot). The dual role of Lizardo/Whorfin gives Lithgow an opportunity to show his versatility, and it's an opportunity that he does not allow to slip from his grasp for even the slightest moment. Lithgow balances the wackiness of a possessed physicist with the manic energy of an alien supervillain. His depiction stands out as both comically exaggerated and genuinely menacing, emphasizing his ability to bring depth to even the most outlandish characters. With his boundless physical energy and brilliant, straight-faced delivery of lines such as "History is-a made at night. Character is what you are in the dark," and "Sealed with a curse as sharp as a knife. Doomed is your soul and damned is your life," Lithgow all but steals the show.

OK, fair enough. He steals the show.

Even for all of Weller's and Lithgow's brilliance, however, we still shouldn't forget the ensemble that provided the film's pulsating heart. First, the love interest. Ellen Barkin's Penny Priddy, initially introduced as a seemingly distressed woman who attempts to shoot herself at a nightclub where Buckaroo Banzai is performing, turns out to be a doppelganger of Buckaroo's deceased wife. Banzai intervenes, saving her, and she's quickly drawn into the film's central plot. As the story unfolds, it's revealed that Penny is actually the long-lost twin sister of Buckaroo's late wife Peggy, which adds an emotional layer to her involvement in the story and gives the movie its romantic heartbeat.

Barkin's portrayal of Penny is characterized by a mix of vulnerability and determination. She effectively captures the essence of a woman thrust into an unexpected, bizarre adventure, all while dealing with the emotional weight of her personal connections to Buckaroo and the discovery of her twin's fate. Barkin provides depth to a character that could easily be relegated to just a romantic subplot, ensuring Penny stands out amidst all the zany people and aliens around her.

Then we have the Hong Kong Cavaliers, the eclectic band and support team of Buckaroo Banzai. The Cavaliers are portrayed by a talented ensemble of actors who each bring their own individuality to the mix. Jeff Goldblum, already well-ensconced in the jittery-cerebral persona that remains his calling card to this day, dons cowboy attire and provides comic relief as New Jersey (a.k.a. Dr. Sidney Zweibel), a neurosurgeon and the most recent recruit to the Cavaliers. Lewis Smith plays Perfect Tommy, the youngest and arguably the slickest member of the group, recognized for his sharp blonde hair and distinctive fashion. Robert Ito takes on the role of Professor Hikita, a close associate of Buckaroo instrumental in crafting the Oscillation Overthruster. Clancy Brown, perhaps better known for playing heavies in movies like *Highlander* and *The Shawshank Redemption,* appears as Rawhide, Buckaroo's loyal right-hand man. Rounding out the Cavaliers are Billy Vera as Pinky Carruthers, the philosophical bass player, and Pepe Serna (*Scarface*) as Reno Nevada. Together, the Cavaliers enhance the film with humor, loyalty and an undeniable sense of camaraderie while they support Buckaroo's interdimensional rock 'n' roll endeavors.

(It's worth noting that in an ironic twist, Vera himself went on to have his own huge real-world '80s pop music hit with *At This Moment*, which had actually been released in 1981 to little fanfare but crashed to the top of the charts a few years later after the song was featured prominently in the Michael J. Fox TV show *Family Ties*.)

Yet for all the acting talent that filled the screen, the existence of *Buckaroo Banzai* is no doubt owed to writer Earl Mac Rauch and director W.D. Richter.

Beyond *Buckaroo*, Richter's most prominent contributions to cinema are as a writer. His résumé boasts credits on genre classics like the 1978 *Invasion of the Body Snatchers* remake, John Badham's *Dracula*, with Fank Langella in the title role (1979) and the adaptation of Stephen King's *Needful Things* (1993). But it's his work on the John Carpenter classic *Big Trouble in Little China* that perhaps hews most closely to the spirit of *Buckaroo Banzai*. The 1986 Carpenter film is every bit *Banzai*'s equal when it comes to its skillfully mixing of genres, this time

into a delightful blend of fantasy/comedy/horror/romance/martial arts/western. Despite displaying such a masterful hand at creating vivid characters and uniquely memorable genre mash-ups, Richter would direct only one more film outside of *Buckaroo Banzai*: the quirky but little-scene science fiction piece *Late for Dinner* (1991). Hollywood is a cruel mistress, indeed.

Earl Mac Rauch's career, on the other hand, is not quite as littered with fan favorites outside of *Buckaroo Banzai*, but it does have its share of interesting variety. Rauch claims three other screenplay credits, the most notable of which by far is his collaboration with Martin Scorsese (!) on the semi-musical *New York, New York*. Yet despite the relative lack of produced credits, by all accounts it is Rauch who is the true originator behind the eccentric world of Buckaroo Banzai.

Richter and Rauch became friends after Richter read and liked Rach's debut novel 'Dirty Pictures from the Prom'. That friendship sparked a creative collaboration that ultimately brought Rauch to Hollywood, and allowed him to create the character of Buckaroo Banzai through a series of stop-and-start attempts. "[He] would get thirty or forty pages into a script, abandon its storyline and write a new one," Richter said in a 1984 interview, while Rauch recalled to John Flynn a decade later in *Across the Eighth Dimension: Remembering the First Adventure of Buckaroo*

Banzai: "It's so easy to start something and then - since you're really not as serious about it as you should be - end up writing half of it... You shove the hundred pages in a drawer and try to forget about it. Over the years, I started a dozen *Buckaroo* scripts that ended that way."

The collaboration between Richter and Rauch on *Buckaroo Banzai* proved to be serendipitous. Behind the scenes, it was magic. Richter's past work, especially his input on *Invasion of the Body Snatchers*, showcased his knack for revitalizing genres. With *Buckaroo Banzai*, he took Rauch's eclectic vision and turned it into a narrative that was as profound as it was entertaining.

Music plays a crucial role in the film, too. Not just in terms of the score, but in the on-screen action too. The Cavaliers *are* a rock band, after all. Weller is on the record as saying he based his performance in part on rocker '80s Adam Ant, and right from the outset, Buckaroo Banzai's multi-dimensional persona is enriched by his identity as a rock musician. One of the early scenes where he performs with his band, the Hong Kong Cavaliers, at a nightclub isn't merely for entertainment. This performance introduces us to the camaraderie between Buckaroo and his bandmates, who aren't just background characters but essential characters in the narrative. They're part of Buckaroo's team; he wouldn't be who he is without them.

The film's atmospheric score, masterfully composed by Michael Boddicker, is as eclectic as its story. It combines

elements of electronic and rock music, mirroring the movie's blend of sci-fi, adventure and comedy. Boddicker's compositions don't merely serve as a backdrop; they accentuate the narrative's turns, amplifying both the high-octane adventure moments and the film's lighter, comedic beats. And of course, there is that end credits music-video sequence, which was dreamed up at the last minute by

Richter but is now recognized as one of *Banzai's* signature moments thanks to the lighthearted and eminently hummable music track.

Yet for all its perfectly mixed ingredients, *The Adventures of Buckaroo Banzai* initially underwhelmed on the financial reports. The majority of audiences didn't seem to get it, and the studio didn't either. The movie split critical opinion; Richard Corliss of 'Time' magazine called it "the very oddest good movie in many a full moon," while 'Variety' noted: "It's hard not to like a film with a hero named Buckaroo Banzai, but it's also hard to like a film that seems to be made up as it goes along." The movie tanked at the box office, earning only $6.2 million in the United States. Not helping matters was that prior to the film's release there was a change in studio leadership at MGM/UA during post-production of the film. The new leadership was reportedly not fond of the movie, which led to limited marketing and a somewhat confusing promotional campaign.

Yet like so many of the science fiction and horror movies we know and love today, initial box office did not doom Buckaroo Banzai, Emilio Lizardo and company to the dustbin of history. Endless cable TV showings and the advent of home video accessibility helped the movie find the grateful audience it deserved. In the years since its release, *The Adventures of Buckaroo Banzai* has become one of the most beloved titles of its genre (of its many genres, that is). In the vast spectrum of '80s sci-fi, *Buckaroo Banzai* stands out not just for its distinctiveness, but for its soul. Amidst the decade's epics, it reminds us of the power of creativity unfettered by conventional expectations. Buckaroo's famous words echo true even today: "Remember, no matter where you go, there you are." It's a testament to the film's enduring spirit, and a reminder to us all to just enjoy ourselves for who we are.

Honor, Duty & Broken Glass

POLICE STORY

by Bryan C. Kuriawa

By 1985, Jackie Chan was one of the world's most prominent action stars. Major successes, including *Drunken Master* (1978), *The Young Master* (1980) and *Project A* (1983), solidified his popularity in Hong Kong, Japan and anywhere his films were imported.

The American market however was a distant dream. Despite efforts, including the Robert Clouse-directed *Battle Creek Brawl* (1980) and a supporting role in the comedy *The Cannonball Run* (1981), he didn't make much headway. While he continued to gain success with Hong Kong and Japanese audiences, it seemed making it in America was an uncertainty. This only intensified in 1985 when Golden Harvest used their contract with Chan to sign him up for the American/Hong-Kong co-production *The Protector*.

Directed by James Glickenhaus (the man behind the 1980 cult classic *The Exterminator*), the film attempted to turn Chan into a hardboiled, swearing '80s action star. Unfortunately, the resulting movie was very mediocre and Chan was not a fan. He would end up making a revised version for Hong Kong audiences with several new scenes featuring actress Sally Yeh and a refilmed final fight. This version also removed the nudity, profanity and more exploitative elements of Glickenhaus' film.

Subsequently, Chan set out to craft his own action epic covering the work of police officers. This production would be the complete antithesis of Glickenhaus' effort.

"These Are Just Fronts to Cover His Main Racket Which is Drugs"

Early one morning, the Royal Hong Kong Police are ready to undertake a special operation in a hillside shantytown. Spearheaded by superintendent Raymond Li (Lam Kwok-Hung), the goal is to apprehend a local businessman Chu Tao (Chor Yuen) who is dealing drugs.

During the operation, Chu's men get wind of the police activity and his secretary Selina Fong (Brigitte Lin) notifies him by telephone. Fong is quickly stopped by a police officer named Ka Kui 'Kevin' Chan (Jackie Chan). In the resulting shootout, multiple officers are injured and Chan chases Chu Tao when he and some of his men escape. He is able to apprehend them after they briefly hijack a local bus.

Despite arresting Chu Tao, Li believes the operation was a mess, failing to gain much hard evidence linking Chu to the drug trade. He decides to enact a new plan involving Miss Fong.

Cancelling the charges against her, he appoints Chan as her bodyguard until she appears in court as a witness for the prosecution. When Chu gets word from his lawyer Peter (Chi-Wing Lau) about Fong's potential defection, he decides he'll need to make appropriate plans. Meanwhile, Chan discovers being Fong's bodyguard is the least of his worries.

A great fusion of action and comedy, *Police Story* is one of the premiere films of '80s Hong Kong cinema. Fusing everything he learned into one production, the result is a movie that turns two genres on their heads.

"No Use Becoming a Police Officer, Not If You Want to Reach a Ripe Old Age"

Following his unpleasant experience on *The Protector*, Chan's goal was to make his own police epic. In the years prior, he worked on period pieces including *Dragon Lord*

(1982) and *Project A* (1983) and modern-day films like *Winners and Sinners* (1983) and the Spain-shot *Wheels on Meals* (1984), the latter two being directed by his close friend and colleague Sammo Hung.

In terms of his work during the '80s, *Police Story* has many familiar faces from his productions during that period including performers such as Mars and Fung-Hark-On, alongside some of Hong Kong's most popular figures including Bill Tung and Brigitte Lin. With a familiar cast and crew, the goal was to unleash the action and the comedy together.

"Please Don't Push Too Hard! You're Going to Break It!"

As this is a film starring, written and directed by Jackie Chan, I should start by discussing how he fares in his performance.

Ka-Kui Chan - also known as Kevin Chan or Jackie Chan (depending on the dub) - is one of his best characters. A loyal Royal Hong Kong policeman, he's a 'superman' in the physical and mental sense of the word. Pushing himself to the limit, he fights and takes abuse to achieve his goals, yet at the same time he's a goofy everyman with a complicated relationship with his whiny, overemotive girlfriend May (Maggie Cheung). He's also prone to complicated problems - for example a multi-phone mess while he's serving at the Hong Kong border police station or when interacting with his superiors.

One of the most popular and famed actresses from Taiwanese and Hong Kong cinema, Lin does a great job as Selina Fong. A brash young woman, Fong is hostile to Chan from their initial interaction during the police operation. This is only enhanced when she discovers Chan faked an intruder-assassination attempt using one of his colleagues (Mars) to scare her. She then sabotages his tape recording of what she said about Chu's activities with inappropriate statements and commentary. Well known for her role in Taiwanese dramas during the '70s, Lin gained more acclaim from her roles in Hong Kong including *Peking Opera Blues* (1986) and the arthouse classic *Chungking Express* (1994). Incidentally, she would play action heroines in numerous films including *Golden Girls Commando* (1982) and the action-comedy *Fantasy Mission Force* (1983), which featured Chan in a supporting role.

More well known as a director in Hong Kong, Chor Yuen portrays a very disgusting figure in Chu Tao, renamed Tom Koo in the original export dub. Self-assured and duplicitous, he views Chan as responsible for his many legal problems. His goal in the film's second half is to make Chan's life a living inferno, using whatever means are available to him.

Maggie Cheung makes a strong impression as Chan's recurring girlfriend May. Yes, the character can be unpleasant, and in the sequel the emphasis on their relationship ruined the film. However, her ability as an actress, the way she makes you hate the character, is in its way a sign of strength. Featuring one of the most seductive British voices, Cheung distinguished herself in multiple films including *The Heroic Trio* (1993) and *In the*

Mood for Love (2000), not to mention working again with Chan on *Project A 2* (1987), *Twin Dragons, Police Story 3: Supercop* (both 1992) and the aforementioned *Police Story 2* (1988).

Many of the supporting performances are also excellent. Whether it's members of Chu's organization or the men in Chan's precinct, they all leave impressions. Of particular note are Bill Tung and Charlie Cho. A popular local racetrack announcer, Tung would become a familiar fixture in multiple future Chan productions including *Miracles* (1989), *Rumble in The Bronx* (1995) and the other *Police Story* entries. His character is a mix of reason and a fun sense of humor. The character also has great comedic timing which transcends several of the English dubs done in Hong Kong.

Portraying Chu's financial brain, Cho's Tom Ko is a similarly reprehensible figure. Helping Chu plot the ruin of Chan using Fong and a corrupt policeman, Sgt. Man (Kam Hing-Yin), he gets one of the funnier outcomes for a cinematic villain. Returning as the same character in *Police Story 2*, Cho was a familiar fixture in 'Category III' softcore erotica films in Hong Kong during the late '80s and '90s. If you want to see films with titles like *Long Hot Summer*, *Unforgettable Holiday* (both 1992) and, amusingly, *Pretty Woman* (1991), there's some interesting eBay searches when looking for overseas film vendors.

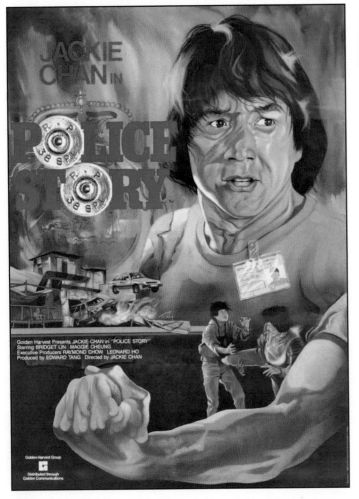

"I Want Kevin Chan to Disappear for Good"

In terms of Chan's prior and subsequent films, *Police Story* is at the center of his evolution as a filmmaker.

In his earlier period works, including *The Young Master* (1980), Chan favored longer takes and scenes, as his fight segments were still making the transition to the pace they would eventually reach. Starting with films like *Project A*, he favored more concise shots with a faster pace and many scenes and set pieces to showcase his team's stunt work, their martial arts abilities and everything in between.

The opening sequence set in the shanty town is a great example of this. Grand in scale, we start with the buildup towards the operation's eventual breakdown. Following the shootout and the destruction of the shantytown by the fleeing crooks, and an in-pursuit Chan, we move to Chan's foot chase and subsequent bus ride, hanging off the side as he tries to get in and is then knocked off. All these moments cascade through their own individual climaxes. Even the more dramatic scenes - such as Chan's court testimony, his moment fighting off Chu's men when he locates a missing Selina, or when he returns to the precinct after being accused of murder - benefit from great setups and tight framing.

This is an action film with a lot of martial arts on display. The action scenes are fast-paced and fluid, showing Chan, his stunt team and their unique brand of fighting. All the fight segments are well composed and spotlight how much Chan and his team members can take in terms of the physical punishment and risk involved.

For those who recall Chan's outtake compilations at the end of his movies, both the original Hong Kong and extended Japanese cuts of this film show the injuries Chan and the team suffered while working on the production. Beyond the individual injuries, the most famous is when three stuntmen went flying through the front of the hijacked bus and landed on the pavement. They were originally supposed to land on the car in front, but the bus had stopped prematurely. In the shot after the fall, you can see Chan continuing the take, while he tries to see what happened to the men.

This climaxes in the final fight scene, where Chan fights Chu's men through a Hong Kong mall after Selina prints a document of all his illegal transactions for the police. Stunt men are smashed into glass, go flying down escalators, onto display counters and even extra-thick jewelry counters. Injuries abound and even Fong becomes part of the mayhem when she's thrown onto a table and subsequently into a display window. The prop glass was made thicker, yet it also caused more injuries.

The amount of broken glass was so much that the film was nicknamed *Glass Story*!

Of course, what's a great fight scene, without a grand climax? We have probably Chan's most famous stunt. Trying to stop Chu from escaping the mall, Chan slides down an electric chandelier and pole, crashing into the kiosk below. As a result of this leap, he dislocated his pelvis and burned all the skin off his hands as well as suffering a back injury and electrocution. Yet, as the final shot of the outtake reel of the extended Japanese cut shows, Chan achieved a great on-screen moment and was on top of the world with the outcome.

Completing the film's strengths are the screenplay and soundtrack. Cowritten by Chan and collaborator Edward Tang, the script manages to maintain a great blend of action, comedy and drama. The underlying message being that of a policeman being pushed to the limits to achieve justice. Chan's character is both an everyman and superman, while his supervisor Raymond is a by-the-book officer. This leads to Ka-Kai confronting him and his inability to see beyond a strict interpretation of the law. By the conclusion, the two are able to reach an understanding and some level of mutual respect, as Raymond's final act shows sympathy with his officer's pursuit.

The soundtrack by composer Michael Lai is excellent and features some great cues. It oscillates between more dramatic pieces and lighter comedic ones, among others. Chan's great theme song *Hero Story* deserves a mention too. For their export cut, Golden Harvest had the film rescored by composer Kevin Bassinson. With some funkier beats and cues, it's a great alternative and was for a long time the most readily available version internationally.

"Jackie Chan is a One-Man Battalion!"

Released in December 1985, *Police Story* was a box-office success for Chan and Golden Harvest. Soon after its release, a full-length English dub was commissioned in Hong Kong under the direction of voice actor Barry Haigh. This dub would be used for the edited export cut and was the best of the four available English options. It was this version that made its American debut at the New York Film Festival in 1987 and was used to create numerous dubs internationally.

Over time, the film's reputation grew, alongside the number of English dubs. New Line Cinema commissioned a second one for their version of the export cut in 1998 for VHS, Laserdisc and American cable TV presentations.

When the movie appeared on DVD, released by Hong Kong Legends in England and Dragon Dynasty in the US, viewers were treated to the third and fourth English dubs. Both completed in Hong Kong, voice actors Rik Thomas and Jack Murphy - known for their work on the English export dubs for '90s and early 2000s *Godzilla* films - could be heard on both tracks. In recent years, the Bassinson-scored export cut and extended Japanese theatrical version appeared on Eureka's British Blu-Ray releases, alongside the uncut original English export dub. The film and its sequel are also available on Blu-ray from the Criterion Collection.

Overall, *Police Story* is an excellent Hong Kong production and one of the best action movies ever. Not only did he top Glickenhaus, he crafted a movie that truly showcased his talent as a director, performer and martial artist. Beloved the world over (as that final shot of Chan after his jump showcases), the film shows that sometimes you need to take a leap.

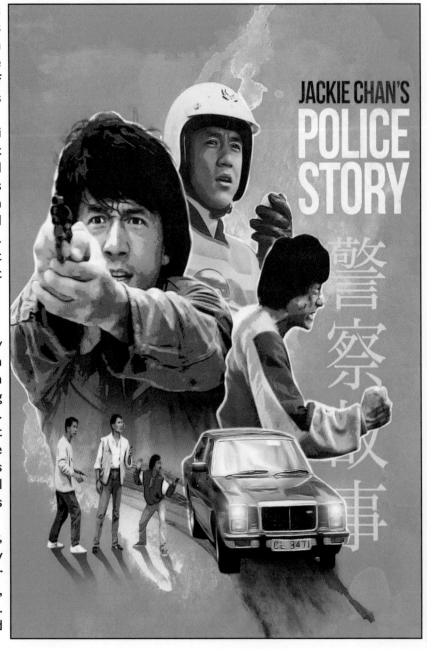

Original Artwork by the Students of Confetti Institute of Creative Technologies

Confetti is a specialist creative technology education provider in Nottingham, England, dealing in fimmaking and VFX, video game design and game art, music production and live performance. The following artwork is original work produced specially for this magazine by students aged 17-18 years.

Beetlejuice by Grace Rawson

Back to the Future by Roxie J

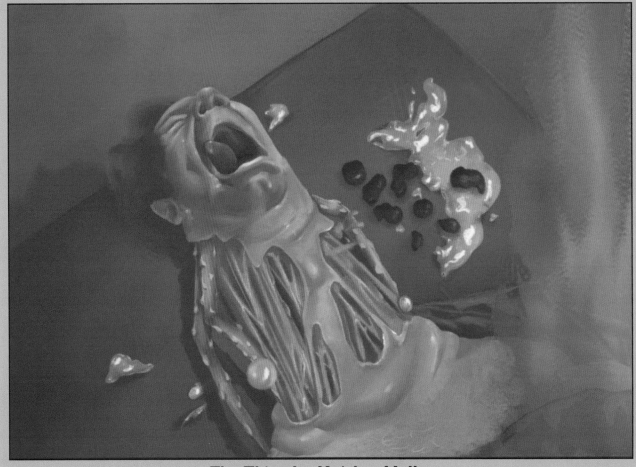

The Thing by Kaitlyn Hallam

CLOSING CREDITS

James Aaron
James is an American writer and film lover living in Kentucky with his wife and two dogs. He is the author (as Aaron Saylor) of three novels, including 'Sewerville' and 'Adventures in Terror', the latter of which is set during the horror movie and video store boom of the 1980s.

Simon J. Ballard
Simon lives in Oxford and works in its oldest building, a Saxon Tower. Whilst also working in the adjoining church, he has never felt tempted to re-enact scenes from *Taste the Blood of Dracula* or *Dracula A.D.1972*. He has never done this. Ever. He regularly contributes to the magazine 'We Belong Dead' and its various publications, and once read Edgar Allan Poe's 'The Black Cat' to a garden full of drunk young people at his local gay pub The Jolly Farmers. His first published work was a Top Tip in 'Viz' of which he is justifiably proud.

Rachel Bellwoar
Rachel is a writer for 'Comicon', 'Diabolique' magazine and 'Flickering Myth'. If she could have any director fim a biopic about her life it would be Aki Kaurismäki.

Michael Campochiaro
Michael is a writer, artist and film and pop culture critic living with his family in New York's Hudson Valley. He has been published in the book 'A Very Special Episode, Volume 1: 1957-1985', in which he wrote about *Taxi* and *WKRP In Cincinnati*. He has written for 'Diabolique Magazine', 'Drive-In Asylum', 'HiLoBrow', 'Grumpire' and more. He is also the biggest Michelle Pfeiffer fan you're likely to meet, so reciting lines from *Grease 2*, *Batman Returns* or other Pfeiffer films is a guaranteed way to earn his loyal friendship.

Sebastian Corbascio
Sebastian is a writer/director and novelist. He was born and raised in Oakland Ca., and lives in Copenhagen, Denmark. His motion picture work can be seen on Youtube/Sebastian Corbascio. His murder mystery novel 'Sarah Luger' can be found on amazon.com. Reach him at facebook.com Sebastian Corbascio

Dawn Dabell
Dawn runs her own clothing business in West Yorkshire. When she's not busy selling fabulous dresses and quirky tops, she's a full-time film enthusiast, writer and mum! She has written for 'Cinema Retro', 'We Belong Dead', 'Monster!' and 'Weng's Chop', and is also the co-author of 'More Than a Psycho: The Complete Films of Anthony Perkins' (2018) and 'Ultimate Warrior: The Complete Films of Yul Brynner' (2019). She is also the co-creator and designer of the very mag you're holding in your hands right now.

Martin Dallard
Fed on a staple diet of the *Six Million Dollar Man*, repeats of the Adam West *Batman* show and the likes of the *Flashing Blade*, and *Champion the Wonder Horse* from a young age, it's no wonder that Martin is self-confessed geek for all things '70s. And whatever you do, don't get him started on the likes of Ron Ely's Doc Savage, as you'll never hear the end of it. Whether it travelled in a TARDIS, or it rode in a red double decker bus, he watched it. But rest assured he never switched off his

David Flack
David was born and bred in Cambridge. Relatively new to the writing game, he has had reviews published in 'We Belong Dead' and 'Cinema of the '70s'. He loves watching, talking, reading and writing about film and participating on film forums. The best film he has seen in over 55 years of watching is *Jaws* (1975). The worst is *The Creeping Terror* (1963) or anything by Andy Milligan.

Shawn Gordon
Shawn has been an avid movie buff since having his fragile little mind warped seeing John Carpenter's *Big Trouble in Little China* and *Highlander* as a double feature at the drive-in when he was six. He is a film critic and historian and former staff writer for 'Movie Zone Magazine', a bi-monthly print and online publication. He is a regular contributor at www.cinapse.co. He has also written for www.horror.com, www.expendablespremiere.com, www.besthorrormovies.com, www.midnightplace.com, www.classic-monsters.com and 'We Belong Dead'. Shawn is a deep believer that *Once Upon a Time in the West* is the greatest movie ever made.

John Harrison

John is a Melbourne, Australia-based freelance writer and film historian who has written for numerous genre publications, including 'Fatal Visions', 'Cult Movies', 'Is It Uncut?', 'Monster!' and 'Weng's Chop'. Harrison is also the author of the Headpress book 'Hip Pocket Sleaze: The Lurid World of Vintage Adult Paperbacks', has recorded audio commentaries for Kino Lorber, and composed the booklet essays for the Australian Blu-ray releases of *Thirst*, *Dead Kids* and *The Survivor*. 'Wildcat!', Harrison's book on the film and television career of former child evangelist Marjoe Gortner, was published by Bear Manor in 2020.

Bryan C. Kuriawa

Based in New Jersey, Bryan has spent many years diving into the world of movies. Introduced to the Three Stooges by his grandfather and Japanese cinema when he was eight, he's wandered on his own path, ignoring popular opinions. Willing to discuss and defend everything from Jesus Franco's surreal outings to the 007 masterpiece *Moonraker*, nothing is off-limits. Some of his favorite filmmakers include Ishiro Honda, Jacques Tati, Lewis Gilbert, Jesus Franco and Jun Fukuda.

James Lecky

James is an actor, writer and occasional stand-up comedian who has had a lifelong obsession with cinema, beginning with his first visit to the Palace Cinema in Derry, (now long since gone) to see *Chitty Chitty Bang Bang* when he was six. Since then, he has happily wallowed in cinema of all kinds but has a particular fondness for Hammer movies, spaghetti westerns, Euro-crime and samurai films.

Ernie Magnotta

Ernie has written for several film magazines such as 'The Dark Side', 'Cinema Retro', 'Rue Morgue' and 'Shock Cinema'. His first book – 'Halloween: The Changing Shape of an Iconic Series' - was released in 2018 and has received rave reviews. His next, titled 'Horror's Sinister Six', will hit bookshelves sometime next year. Ernie currently lives in New York.

Peter Sawford

Peter was born in Essex in 1964 so considers himself a child of the '70s. A self-confessed film buff, he loves watching, reading about and talking about cinema. A frustrated writer his whole life, he's only recently started submitting what he writes to magazines. His favourite director is Alfred Hitchcock with Billy Wilder running him a close second. He still lives in Essex with his wife and works as an IT trainer and when not watching films he's normally panicking over who West Ham are playing next.

Joseph Secrett

Joseph is a film nut and collector who started at a young age, and quickly became infatuated with all things cinematic. He is a huge fan of 20th century cinema, especially the '60s and '70s for their sheer diversity of genres. Top choices of his include revisionist westerns and seedy crime dramas.

Ian Talbot Taylor

After early short story successes, Ian began editing music fanzines and spent decades acting, directing and adjudicating in amateur theatre for the Greater Manchester Drama Federation. He writes for 'The Dark Side', 'Infinity', 'Scream', 'Fantastic Fifties', 'Halls of Horror' and 'We Belong Dead' (and is on the editorial team of the latter). His book on the films of Jenny Agutter appeared in 2021. Ian has progressed from 'prose dabbler' to prolific fiction writer, contributing to and co-editing the BHF Books of Horror. He recently released the collaborative fiction collection 'Spoken in Whispers' and also presents shows for Radio M29 .

Dr. Andrew C. Webber

Dr. W, a film teacher and examiner for over 35 years, already writes passionately for 'Cinema of the '70s' magazine and also contributes to the cassette gazette fanzine. He pontificates about music on the Low Noise podcast (available on Apple and Spotify) and his blogs can occasionally be found on Oxford's Ultimate Picture Palace cinema website. He still loves being "at" the movies and would describe himself as a lover of cinema, if asked.

Printed in Great Britain
by Amazon